PUBLICATIONS OF THE
FOUNDATION FOR FINNISH ASSYRIOLOGICAL RESEARCH
NO. 33

STATE ARCHIVES OF ASSYRIA CUNEIFORM TEXTS
VOLUME XIII

State Archives of Assyria Cuneiform Texts (SAACT) is a series of text editions presenting central pieces of Mesopotamian literature both in cuneiform and in transliteration, with complete glossaries, name indexes and sign lists generated electronically from the transliterations. The goal of the series is to eventually make the entire library of Assurbanipal available in this format.

Published with the support of the
Foundation for
Finnish Assyriological Research

Set in Times
Typesetting by Geraldina Rozzi and Mikko Luukko
Software development by Iikka Hauhio
Cover layout by Kati Lehtonen, Unigrafia, Helsinki
The Assyrian Royal Seal emblem drawn by Dominique Collon from original
Seventh Century B.C. impressions (BM 84672 and 84677) in the British Museum
Cover: Embroideries on the breast of a king (reign of Assurnasirpal II). Layard,
Monuments of Nineveh I, Pl. 6

Printed in the USA
Distributed by Eisenbrauns,
an imprint of Penn State University Press

ISBN 978-951-51-8586-0 (Volume 13)
ISSN 1455-2345 (SAACT)
ISSN 1798-7431 (PFFAR)

STATE ARCHIVES OF ASSYRIA
CUNEIFORM TEXTS

VOLUME XIII

THE GREAT HYMN TO ŠAMAŠ

By
Geraldina Rozzi

With a Translation of the Hymn by
Benjamin R. Foster

THE NEO-ASSYRIAN TEXT CORPUS PROJECT
2026

ACKNOWLEDGMENTS

This book is based on the online edition I prepared for the Electronic Babylonian Literature project (eBL) in 2021. My work with eBL has given me the opportunity to study newly discovered manuscripts and enabled me to update and extend W.G. Lambert's seminal edition of the text. I am deeply indebted to the many scholars who have contributed to this work.

First and foremost, I would like to thank the eBL team: Enrique Jiménez (PI), Aino Hätinen, Zsombor Földi, Adrian Heinrich and Tonio Mitto. Their insightful feedback and suggestions have greatly improved this edition and aided my interpretation of the text. I am particularly grateful to E. Jiménez and Anmar Fadhil for their kind permission to include two unpublished manuscripts in the transliteration. These manuscripts will be published by E. Jiménez and A. Fadhil in due course. Special thanks are due to T. Mitto for reading the manuscript and providing valuable comments and support.

My thanks also go to Simo Parpola for his generous support in enabling me to publish this volume in the SAACT series. Moreover, I am grateful to Amar Annus, who did some of the groundwork for publishing the Šamaš Hymn himself, for suggesting and encouraging me to publish the hymn in the SAACT series and for putting me in touch with Simo Parpola. I also wish to express my gratitude to Mikko Luukko for his patient and invaluable editorial assistance. His help in revising this book was indispensable.

I would also like to thank the following people. Selim Adalı gave me access to an unpublished fragment that he intends to publish within the İstanbul Sippar Project. Benjamin Foster engaged with me in many fruitful discussions on the interpretation of this challenging text, as well as offering keen insights and advice and allowing me to include his translation in this book. Christopher Metcalf also provided useful references and valuable comments. Moreover, I thank Lorenzo Verderame and Ivan Hrůša, who supervised my Master's thesis and guided me as I first engaged with this text. Julian Reade was a great help in choosing the cover illustration.

In addition, I am sincerely grateful to Daniel Schwemer and my colleagues at the University of Würzburg for their unwavering support and for fostering a peaceful and stimulating environment in which to complete this book. In particular, I would like to thank Henry Lewis and Helen Young for reading parts of the manuscript and carefully revising the English. I also thank Beatrice Baragli for our many enriching conversations about the Mesopotamian Sun God, and Johannes Bach for his insightful feedback on the introduction to the volume.

All mistakes remain my own.

Würzburg, November 2024 Geraldina Rozzi

CONTENTS

INTRODUCTION

Akkadian literature encompasses numerous compositions that can aptly be defined as "hymns," under the classical categorization of literary genres.[1] Hymns, by definition, are compositions directed towards deities (or, more generally, towards superior beings), with their primary purpose being the expression of praise and reverence for the invoked divine entity.[2] The development of Akkadian hymns can be traced back to the Old Babylonian period, coinciding with the decline of Sumerian language, which provided fertile ground for Akkadian literary compositions to flourish.[3] Akkadian hymns exhibit certain formal traits and content parallels with prayers. However, they can be distinguished from prayers in that they place a greater emphasis on the element of praise and less emphasis on petition.[4] Among Akkadian compositions of these genres, scholars identify one specific group of texts as Great Hymns and Prayers.[5] This corpus consists of several compositions which display both stylistic and conceptual sophistication (see *infra*).

---

[1] The difficulty in identifying the literary genres of cuneiform texts lies in the lack of emic definitions (on the problem of genre in Mesopotamian texts, see the brief overview in Lenzi 2019, 37-38, with previous literature). Nevertheless, employing western definitions, occasionally borrowed from Classical literature, can be useful for better understanding the differences and similarities between Mesopotamian literary texts (see Reiner 1991, 293-294). Moreover, although there is no native nomenclature, some definitions provided by the Mesopotamians themselves can offer valuable insights into the context and use of texts. Specifically, regarding hymns, several terms are used that seem to define, if not an entire literary genre, at least different types of hymns. Most of these terms originate from Sumerian and relate to the manner of recitation and musical accompaniment. For example, subscripts such as adab or tigi for Sumerian hymns (Metcalf 2015, 17-18; cf. Shehata 251-257), or šer$_3$/*zamār tanittim* and *pārum* for Akkadian ones; or rubrics such as kirugu or gešgigal in both Sumerian and Akkadian compositions (Metcalf 2015, 53-57; cf. Shehata 2009, 307-326). Note that the term *zamāru*, "song", was also applied to epic compositions (e.g. Enūma eliš and Erra), a fact which highlights once again the difficulty of applying Western concepts and categories to Sumerian-Akkadian literature (see Westenholz 1999, 87; Oshima 2011, 33-37). Thus far, no manuscript of the *Great Hymn to Šamaš* contains a rubric or a subscript.

[2] For a general definition of hymns, see Knittel and Kording 2013. https://doi.org/10.1515/hwro.4.hymne. Accessed 2024-08-03. Cf. also Furley and Bremer 2001, 1-2, who mention the setting in which hymns might take place, e.g. temples or shrines.

[3] Metcalf 2015, 50.

[4] For Akkadian hymns, see von Soden 1972-1975, 544-548; cf. Wilcke 1972-75 for Sumerian hymns; cf. also Metcalf 2015 for a comparison between Akkadian, Sumerian and Indoeuropean hymns. For a recent treatment of Old Babylonian Hymns, see Pohl 2022. For Old Babylonian hymns as a genre, see Streck 2020, with previous literature; the latter study also illustrates the difference between Akkadian hymns and prayers, and between Akkadian hymns and epic (Streck 2020, 660-661).

[5] The label of "Great Hymns and Prayers" was used by Foster 2005, 583-635, and Foster 2007, 78-82. This group of texts now includes 9 compositions: the *Great Hymn to Šamaš*, the *Gula*

The *Great Hymn to Šamaš* also falls within this group of texts. At 200 lines long, it exhibits exceptional stylistic and poetic complexity, with a large portion in the middle devoted to the themes of wisdom and ethics. In addition, this hymn is one of the most widely transmitted literary works in Mesopotamia, copies of which are attested from the ninth to the first century BCE in both Assyria and Babylon.

Brünnow (1889, 1-35) provided the first edition of two Nineveh fragments (NinNA1 and NinNA2a), but the first comprehensive edition of the hymn can be found in Lambert's seminal *Babylonian Wisdom Literature* (*BWL*, 1960).[6] This was followed by the edition of a further manuscript of the text from Sippar, provided by George and Al-Rawi (1996). In 1997, Geller published a small fragment of a late Babylonian school tablet, where an extract from the *Great Hymn to Šamaš* was preserved.[7] Copies of additional fragments were published in the first volume of the series *Cuneiform Texts from the Folios of W. G. Lambert* (*CTL*) by George and Taniguchi in 2019.

In 2021, a digital edition of the hymn was released on *eBL* (Rozzi 2021a)[8]. Subsequently, previously unedited fragments were also published individually by Rozzi 2021b, 2022b, 2023. The text has been translated into various languages, the main translations being Seux (1976), Castellino (1977, 383-392), Reiner (1985, 68-84), Foster (2005, 627-635), and Hecker (2013, 66-72).[9]

The Sun God Šamaš

Šamaš, known as Utu in Sumerian, was the Mesopotamian Sun God, worshipped primarily in the southern Babylonian cities of Larsa and Sippar, but as one of the

---

Hymn of Bullussa-rabi, the *Hymn to the Queen of Nippur* (to Ištar), the *Great Prayer to Ištar*, the *Prayer to Anūna* (to Ištar of Babylon), the *Great Prayer to Marduk* (Marduk 1), the *Great Hymn to Marduk* (Marduk 2), the *Great Prayer to Nabû*, and the *Syncretistic Hymn to Gula*. The updated edition of all these texts, except Marduk 1, Marduk 2 and the Prayer to Anuna (edited by Lenzi at http://akkpm.org/P269974.html), can be found on the platform of the electronic Babylonian Library project (eBL), where previous bibliographic references are included. The definition of the corpus of the Great Hymns and Prayers provided here is purely formal and subject to revision. This corpus is not definitive, and future discoveries will likely bring to light new texts. For a study on the whole corpus, with comprehensive editions of the Great Prayer to Nabû and the Great Prayer to Ištar, see Rozzi 2024a.

[6] Other partial editions are Gray 1901a, 129-145 and 242; Gray 1901b, 9-24 with plates 1-2 (part of NinNA1 and NinNA3a); Schollmeyer 1912, 80-93 (NinNA1); Schollmeyer 1952-53, 46 with plates 7-8 (SipNB3a). Ebeling (1923) provided a copy of AššNASch1 (KAR 321). For more earlier literature, including partial translations, see Lambert 1960a, 124.

[7] Geller 1997, 78 and 94.

[8] This book is based on the online edition, accessible from the eBL platform: https://www.ebl.lmu.de/corpus/L/3/4, last accessed 08.08.2024. The eBL edition provides the synoptic transliteration of the hymn, photos of the manuscripts (when available) and philological notes.

[9] See Foster 2005, 635 for further studies on the hymn.

greatest gods in the pantheon, he was also worshipped in many other Babylonian and Assyrian shrines throughout the long history of Mesopotamia.[10] He was the son of the Moon God Sin and the goddess Ningal, and the brother of Ištar/Inanna.[11]

Beyond his solar qualities as the illuminator of darkness, Šamaš possessed additional prerogatives. He traveled over the earth in his horse-drawn chariot[12], traversing both hemispheres (upper and lower) and even reaching the Netherworld.[13] This omnipresence rendered Šamaš omniscient; he saw and knew everything. Due to his omniscience, he served as the judge of gods and men, guaranteeing truth and order in the world. During his journey, Šamaš also visited the Netherworld, acting as judge of the dead. Hence, he played a crucial role in the Mesopotamian cult of the dead.[14]

Šamaš's role in maintaining order and justice in both the upper and lower worlds was reflected in his prominence in religious rituals and divinatory practices. He was invoked to ensure the proper conduct of these practices in order to secure truthful outcomes. Moreover, the very nature of the god – eternal, omniscient, and unchanging – lent itself to his role as a messenger of future events.[15]

At the end of his daily journey, before the dawning of a new day, Šamaš returned to his dwelling,[16] where he was welcomed by his wife (Aya in Akkadian, Šerda in Sumerian; cf. ll. 199-200 of the hymn under consideration).[17] Šamaš was

---

[10] For a general description on the Mesopotamian Sun God, see Krebernik 2009-2011, 599-611, 605-606; Krebernik 2019, 66-68; cf. also Hrůša 2015, 48-49. A temple of Šamaš is also attested at the end of the first millennium in the city of Hatra. On the cult of Šamas in Hatra, see Kubiak-Schneider 2022. Cf. also Steitler 2017 for attestation of the Sun God cult in Anatolia.

[11] Krebernik 2009-2011, 602-603; Hrůša 2015, 48. Cf. Baragli 2022a, 95-105, for a detailed description of the minor deities or semi-divine entities, who accompany Utu on his journey, including the horses that pull the Sun God's chariot.

[12] Alaura and Bonechi 2012, 5-115.

[13] For this description of the Mesopotamian cosmic geography, see Steinkeller 2005, 18-21; cf. Baragli 2022a, 109-110.

[14] For a comprehensive account of the role of the Sun God in the cult of the dead, both from a mythological and ritualistic perspective, see Baragli 2022a, 117-120, with further references.

[15] Steinkeller 2005, 34-36. In particular, see 35: "However, the connection between the future and the sun god is even more immediate and intimate since, being identical with the sun god *is* the future. At night, when he passes through the netherworld, he is potential future, an infinite sequence of days to come. At daybreak, when he returns to the upper world, he becomes the future realized."

[16] The bedchamber of the Sun God is called agrun in Sumerian and *kummu* in Akkadian. Some scholars assume that this is where the Sun God sleeps (e.g., Heimpel 1986, 129), although this interpretation is rejected by others (e.g., Steinkeller 2005, 25 with fn. 36). See Baragli 2022a, 599 fn. 19, for further references. For the concept of the bedchamber of the Sun God, see also the Sumerian literary composition recently published by Peterson and Baragli (2024), i 20′ ki-nú ... gub ("to set up a bedchamber"), Peterson and Baragli 2024, 27 and 42-43. For further attestations of the chamber of the Sun God, and its ambiguous location, cf. also the discussion in Polonsky 2002, 190-192.

[17] Regarding the daily path of the sun, see Heimpel 1986 and Baragli 2022a, 107-12. There appear to be various traditions, sometimes conflicting with each other. This especially concerns the ambiguity of certain terms, such as the so-called "heaven's interior" (Sum. an-šà, Akk. *qereb šamê*). The "heaven's interior" is a place through which the Sun God passes during his journey. Some scholars argue that this is where the agrun/*kummu* is located (Heimpel 1986, 129).

also the protector of various categories of people: travelers, merchants, and, in general, people in difficult situations – the abandoned, the poor, orphans, widows, the homeless, exiles, prisoners, the sick, and others. As a light-bearer, Šamaš regulated the seasons and guaranteed the order of nature, extending his influence over the animal world as well.[18]

The figure of Šamaš appears in a wide range of textual sources[19] that have come down to us from the third millennium BCE up to the end of cuneiform culture. Attestations of Šamaš are found, for example, in lexical lists (such as god lists of the type An = Anum[20]), and in administrative texts (e.g., Neo-Babylonian texts mentioning the chariot of the Sun God[21]). Šamaš is also frequently mentioned in literary compositions and ritual texts.

Mentions of Šamaš/Utu occur in several myths and epics, although Šamaš does not typically appear as a protagonist. The Sun God is mainly invoked through a variety of Emesal lamentations (including few Eršema and Balaĝ compositions), royal hymns, temple hymns involving the Sun God's temple (the Ebabbar), letter-prayers, incantations, incantation-prayers and other sorts of prayers.[22]

Some *Zame* Hymns in Sumerian, composed for the temple of Utu and found at Abu Salabikh, date from the third millennium BCE.[23] Several hymns to Utu in Sumerian can be dated to the Old Babylonian period.[24] Additionally, there are compositions from this period that can be considered as straddling the categories of hymns and incantations, namely the Šernamšub and Šergida.[25] From the Old

---

According to other interpretations, the "heavens' interior" can be defined as the region of the sky below the horizon from which the sun rises, and into which it sets at the end of the day (Baragli 2022a, 109, following Steinkeller 2005). Other scholars maintain that Šamaš traverses the underworld during the night (see Heimpel 1986, 127 with fn. 2); it has also been suggested, that the "heaven's interior" might be located in the underworld, e.g., Shibata 2008, 192; according to Shibata, the house of the Sun God is also in the underworld (*loc. cit.*). See Alaura and Bonechi 2002, 50-51, with fn. 223 for a summary of the different hypotheses. For a discussion on the apparent contradictions in Mesopotamian sources regarding the sun's activities at night, see Heimpel (1986, 146-151), who argues that the inconsistencies are merely the result of different traditions. Baragli (2022a), however, commenting on the supposed contradiction involving the presence of the sun in the underworld (famously described as a place devoid of light), contends that it is a metaphor: what reaches the underworld is the sunlight in a metaphorical sense, i.e., the light of Šamaš's justice and an extension of his power.

[18] Both in Sumerian and Akkadian sources, see Baragli 2022a, 107-108.

[19] For archaeological and iconographical records, see Kurmangaliev 2009-2011. Šamaš is usually depicted with the symbol of the solar disk (a four-pointed star from which waving lines emanate, representing the sunrays), cf. Black-Green 1998, 168. Cf. Hrůša 2015, 48. For a history of the evolution of the sun disk in Mesopotamia, see Seidl 2020.

[20] Krebernik 2009-2011, 606.

[21] Alaura and Bonechi 2012, 6.

[22] For a list of the textual sources in which the Sun God is attested, see Krebernik 2009-2011, Polonsky 2002, 49–52. Cf. Baragli 2022b, 322. See also the project "Sources of Early Akkadian Literature" (SEAL) at www.seal.uni-leipzig.de, where the updated editions of further literary texts concerning Šamaš from the third and second millennia BCE are available.

[23] Bauer, Englund and Krebernik 1998, 320. For a recent treatment of the *Zame* Hymns, see Krebernik and Lisman 2020.

[24] Baragli 2022b.

[25] Baragli 2022a, 143-144, with previous literature.

Babylonian period, we also have many Sumerian incantations, though their number begins to decline from the Middle Babylonian period onwards. Among the most important compositions involving Utu/Šamaš in Sumerian are the incantation-prayers known as ki-^{d}utu (Kiutu).[26]

The first literary text written in a Semitic language addressed to the Sun God is an archaic hymn from the third millennium BCE, found at Abu Salabikh, with a duplicate found at Ebla.[27] As the use of Sumerian declined, prayers to Šamaš began to proliferate in both Sumerian-Akkadian and in Akkadian only. While Akkadian or bilingual prayers to the Sun God are numerous, hymns are relatively few in comparison.[28]

Outside of Mesopotamia proper, noteworthy are three rather damaged Akkadian hymns to Šamaš found at Ugarit[29] and an Akkadian hymn-prayer found at Ortaköy (ancient Šapinuwa), recently edited by Schwemer and Süel (2021).[30] The Ortaköy composition closely parallels both the Hittite Prayers to the Sun God (CTH 372-74; Rieken et al. 2017; Schwemer 2015) and their earlier Sumerian model, the hymn Utu ur-saĝ Utu máš-saĝ (Cavigneaux 2009).[31]

In the first millennium, Šamaš held an important role in divinatory practices, as can be seen in the many divination queries presented to Šamaš, most of which date from the reign of Esarhaddon[32], and in rituals, as evidenced by the numerous anti-witchcraft rituals addressed to the Sun God.[33] Anti-witchcraft ritual texts included prayers, which in some cases were originally used for other purposes (e.g., Šu'ila prayers), and were later incorporated into the ritual. Numerous first-

---

[26] Baragli 2022a, 125.

[27] Lambert 1989 and 1992; Krebernik 1992, 81-86; Krebernik 1998, 320; see also Foster 2005, 50-51; on the Ebla parallel, cf. Bonechi 2024.

[28] Krebernik 2009-2011, 607-609.

[29] Arnaud 2007, 103-110.

[30] There are three more compositions from Boğazköy addressed to the Sun God: an Akkadian hymn preserved on a two-column tablet, with a Hittite translation on the second column (KBo 1.12, CTH 792.1), which has a partial parallel in an Assur text (VAT 9302, KAR 19, see Ebeling 1954 for the edition of both texts, cf. more recently Bawanypeck 2014, 83); a poorly preserved Akkadian prayer that was probably used in rituals (KBo 9.44, CTH 792.2; see Bawanypeck 2014, 83-84); and a bilingual composition (Sumerian-Akkadian) which is possibly a Kiutu prayer (CTH 793; KUB 4.11; see Baragli 2022a, 229ff. for the identification of CTH 793 as a Kiutu prayer). For a general overview of Akkadian texts in Anatolia, see Giusfredi, Pisaniello and Matessi 2023, 206-241.

[31] In fact, the similarity in motifs and themes between Utu ur-saĝ Utu máš-saĝ, the Akkadian hymn-prayer from Ortaköy and the group of prayers CTH 372-74 seems to corroborate Metcalf's reconstruction of the overall textual history of the earliest Hittite prayers. This reconstruction assumes the involvement of Akkadian intermediaries in composing and transmitting the Hittite texts. The Ortaköy hymn-prayer to the Sun God probably represents an example of these intermediaries, constituting the Akkadian link between the OB Sumerian hymn and the later Hittite prayers CTH 372-74. On this see Metcalf 2011; 2015b; 2023; cf. Schwemer and Süel 2021, 18 and Schwemer forthcoming.

[32] Starr 1990, see xiii-xiv. Cf. also the corpus of oracle questions, i.e. the so-called *tamītu*-texts, preserved in manuscripts all dating to the first millennium BCE. In the *tamītu*-texts, Šamaš is paired with Adad, the two gods forming a divine duo (see Lambert 2007).

[33] For a collection of anti-witchcraft rituals addressing Šamaš, see CMAwR 1-3.

millennium incantations comprised prayers to Šamaš, mostly written in Akkadian, and more rarely bilingual.[34]

From the same period royal hymns such as one dedicated to Šamaš for Ashurbanipal and a prayer for Nebuchadnezzar II are documented.[35]

However, none of these hymns or prayers in Akkadian can be considered of a standard comparable to the one presented here. This text is distinctive in view of a number of unique features, which will be discussed in the following sections.

The Šamaš Hymn as a Literary Classic

The Hymn to Šamaš shares certain themes and formulae with other Akkadian hymns and prayers addressed to the Sun God. However, it stands out due to several remarkable characteristics. First, its exceptional length and complex poetic structure set it apart. Additionally, it is notable for the large number of copies which have survived in both Babylonian and Assyrian manuscripts, spanning from at least the seventh century BCE to as late as the first century BCE. Furthermore, this hymn is distinguished from other compositions to Šamaš by its unique format, since many of its manuscripts are organized into couplets separated by horizontal rulings. This format aligns the text with other Great Hymns and Prayers.[36] This group of compositions, currently comprising nine texts (including five hymns and four prayers[37]), is distinguished by its high poetic quality, which employs the so-called "Hymno-Epic" Dialect (see *infra*) and various rhetorical devices. Occasionally, these texts also engage in philosophical reflections on human existence and suffering.

Other notable examples within this category include lengthy prayers dedicated to Nabû[38] and Marduk (with the latter text referred to by modern scholars as Marduk 1), and a literary hymn praising Marduk (known as Marduk 2).[39]

The Hymn to Šamaš demonstrates a close relationship with Marduk 1 and Marduk 2. Indeed, in addition to the intertextual connections between the three

---

[34] See for example K 2563+, an Akkadian incantation-prayer addressed to the Sun God and used during the second house of the *Bīt rimki* ritual, see Abusch and Schwemer 2011, 19-20, and 376-386.

[35] Foster, 2005, 827-828, 848.

[36] For more on the format and other material characteristics of manuscripts of Akkadian hymns and prayers, see Rozzi 2024b.

[37] See above fn. 5 for the list of the Great Hymns and Prayers.

[38] Von Soden 1971; cf. also the digital edition in Rozzi 2021a. A new edition is available in Rozzi 2024a.

[39] For the most recent edition of Marduk 1 and Marduk 2, see Oshima 2011. An additional fragment was recently published by Fadhil and Jiménez 2019. A new edition of both texts is in preparation by E. Jiménez.

texts[40], several manuscripts of Marduk 1 preserve the opening line of the Hymn to Šamaš as a catchline.[41] Furthermore, a Nineveh manuscript of The Hymn to Šamaš (K 3182+ iv 34, NinNA1) incorporates the catchline of another literary composition, possibly the so-called "A Hymn in praise of Babylon and the Babylonians", i.e., another hymnic composition involving the god Marduk.[42]

In this context, it is remarkable that the Great Hymn to Šamaš seems to be one of the few literary compositions studied in the first-millennium school curriculum, both in Assyria and Babylonia, that is not addressed to Marduk and does not feature him in a central role.[43] The numerous school fragments that preserve The Hymn to Šamaš also reveal regional preferences, or at the very least, tendencies. In Babylon, extracts from this hymn were frequently copied together with extracts from *Enūma eliš* (typically one immediately following the other, see e.g., manuscript SipNBSch2, SipNBSch1, BabLBSch14). In Assur, on the other hand, they were also combined with *Ludlul* and *Erra*. The *Great Hymn to Šamaš* was thus incorporated into the so-called "Marduk Syllabus", comprising a group of compositions involving Marduk, that was particularly popular in northern Babylonian school tablets.[44] In addition, the Šamaš Hymn is quoted in

[40] See the commentary to ll. 17, 18 and 198 for some parallels between the *Great Hymn to Šamaš* and Marduk 2.

[41] Lambert 1960b, 48; cf. Fadhil and Jiménez 2019, 171.

[42] See Fadhil and Jiménez 2024. The sequence suggested by Fadhil and Jiménez would be then: Marduk 1, Hymn to Babylon, *Great Hymn to Šamaš*. This is not the only instance of a connection among the Great Hymns and Prayers through catchlines. Indeed, a manuscript of the *Gula Hymn of Bullussa-rabi* (BM 33849+BM 47756) also preserves a catchline that corresponds to the first line of the *Syncretistic Hymn to Gula* (see the edition of this manuscript of the *Gula Hymn of Bullussa-rabi* in Földi forthcoming; a more detailed discussion on the catchline of the *Syncretistic Gula Hymn*, with a reconstruction of the first lines of the composition, will appear in a forthcoming publication by Bennett; cf. also Földi 2022b, in which the incipit of the *Syncretistic Hymn to Gula* is erroneously understood as the beginning of an unpublished hymn to Zarpanītu).

[43] The literary texts that appear most frequently on first-millennium school fragments, and which can therefore be considered "classics" of Babylonian literature, are the Great Hymn to Šamaš, *Ludlul*, *Enūma eliš*, the literary prayer to Marduk (Marduk 1), the hymn to Marduk (Marduk 2), the series of incantations *Marduk's Address to the Demons*, the *Aluzinnu Text*, *Counsels of Wisdom* and a hymn to Babylon (labelled by scholars *A Hymn in Praise of Babylon and the Babylonians*), which was recently identified by E. Jiménez, and is now comprehensively published for the first time by A. Fadhil and E. Jiménez 2024. On the most copied texts in the Babylonian school curriculum, cf. also George 2003, 36. Note that all the texts mentioned here are centered on the figure of Marduk, except for *Aluzinnu*, *Counsels of Wisdom*, and the *Great Hymn to Šamaš*.

[44] On different Babylonian school curricula and the "Marduk Syllabus", see Jiménez and Heidrich 2021, 164: "Similar local preferences are also observable in the northern Babylonian curriculum, which is heavily focused on what one may style the "Marduk Syllabus" (*Enūma eliš*, *Ludlul*, *Marduk's Address*, and the Prayers to Marduk I and II), texts entirely absent from southern Babylonian school tablets."

commentaries from Babylon and Sippar[45], further indicating its prominence and frequent use in scribal education.[46]

It is difficult to find a clear and definitive explanation for this phenomenon. The two deities, Marduk and Šamaš, shared similar characteristics: while Šamaš's primary quality was justice and Marduk's his compassion for mankind, both deities were revered as protectors and helpers of the downtrodden.[47] This is also evident in private texts, such as letters, where the names of both gods are often mentioned together in the request for well-being and favour.[48] In the Neo-Babylonian period in Sippar, a certain syncretism between Šamaš and Marduk can be observed in cultic practice, in that the recitation of Balaĝ-lamentations to Marduk took place as part of the liturgy of the Sippar temple.[49]

However, although the two gods may have displayed similar characteristics, it is possible that the popularity of the *Great Hymn to Šamaš* within the more advanced phase of scribal education, as attested in both Assyrian and Babylonian school tablets, did not have much to do with religious practices and syncretistic traditions. Rather, it might simply have been a result of the important theological and ethical themes which this hymn contains, and of its style, which includes numerous poetic embellishments and a refined vocabulary.[50]

Content and Structure

In terms of content, the *Great Hymn to Šamaš* displays some interesting features, which are further enhanced by its use of sophisticated stylistic and poetic elements. It includes themes commonly found in other hymns and prayers addressed to

---

[45] The hymn is quoted in two commentaries on the medical series Sagig (BM 40837 from Babylon and BM 66965+ from Sippar, both Sagig IV) and in a commentary on *Iqqur īpuš* (BM 92705). For more on these manuscripts, see Rozzi 2021a with further references.

[46] Cf. also Jiménez and Heidrich 2021, 164 fn. 10, on the transmission of *Lugale* and its citation in commentaries.

[47] Sommerfeld 1982, 123-124; Baragli 2022a, 113.

[48] Sommerfeld 1982, 121-126.

[49] Note, however, that in the Šamaš temple in Sippar, Emesal prayers to other gods were also recited before the statue of the Sun God. See Maul 1999, 306-309; Gabbay 2014, 108-109. Cf. also Lambert 2013, 163f.

[50] The didactic significance of the Šamaš Hymn is particularly emphasized in a school tablet from Assur (VAT 10174), where the selection of text excerpts from the *A Hymn in Praise of Babylon and the Babylonians*, Marduk 2, the Šamaš Hymn, and the *Erra Epic* suggests a purposeful design. The excerpts preserved in this school tablet highlight fundamental themes, suggesting that all these texts, including the Šamaš Hymn, served not only as literary exercises but also as theological tools. Indeed, the passages in VAT 10174 provide students with reflective content that explores the nature of divine-human relationships, focusing on key themes such as justice, grace, and punishment. In this context, the Šamaš Hymn likely played a crucial role in fostering theological reflection among budding scribes. On this see Maul and Manasterska 2023, 115.

Šamaš, and thus aligns with the traditional theology of the Sun God. Nevertheless, it also displays several formulations that differ from the conventional form of a hymn, being more akin to those of a wisdom text. Furthermore, the Šamaš Hymn shows intertextual parallels with other literary compositions (see *infra*: *Themes, Literary Motifs, and Wisdom*).

The structure of the hymn is noteworthy: as scholars have stated in previous studies of the text, the hymn exhibits a ring structure[51], while still displaying most of the structural characteristics typical of Akkadian hymns.

Akkadian hymns mirror the tripartite format of Sumerian hymns, typically composed of an initial section in which the deity being addressed is invoked (*invocatio*), a central section in which praises to the deity are developed (*laudatio*), and a conclusion (*salutatio*), which may also include a brief prayer section (*preces*).[52] Often, the *invocatio* in Akkadian hymns is developed through the repetition of two almost identical couplets, distinguished only by the delayed introduction of the god's name in the second set. This form is known as the *a-a'* repetition and is borrowed from the Sumerian model.[53] Occasionally, Akkadian hymns mention how the invoked god was endowed with their qualities and prerogatives by other gods. This element is called *elatio.*[54] Traditionally, Akkadian hymns do not contain narrative passages; instead, they consist predominantly of praises and, to a much lesser extent, prayers. This is in contrast to Greek hymns, such as the Homeric Hymns, which often include narrative elements. There are, however, a few exceptions to the general rule.[55]

In the *elatio*-section, the Akkadian hymns tend to make use of the so-called '"Ich will preisen"-Formel', also named "Let me sing"-phrase, a formula in which

---

[51] A "ring structure", or "ring composition", is a literary structure that starts with a particular theme, elaborates on it in the following discussion, and then returns to the initial theme at the end. This approach creates a symmetrical and unified section, making it distinct from the surrounding text. For more on this device, see Engels 2013. For the ring-structure of the Šamaš Hymn, see Castellino 1976 and Reiner 1985, 68-84.

[52] I borrow these terms from Metcalf 2015b; the same terminology used to describe the structure of Old Babylonian hymns is retained in Pohl 2022. This structure is not unique to Sumerian-Akkadian hymns, but is attested in many other ancient literatures, such as Ancient Greek and Hittite. On this see Metcalf 2015b.

[53] On this kind of repetition, see Metcalf 2015, 22-23, for the Sumerian sources, and 62-63 for the Akkadian ones. This rhetorical device is not exclusive to the hymnic genre, though it is perhaps more common in hymns. For example, it can also be found in prayers, such as in Marduk 1, ll. 1-4 (see Oshima 2011, 142, 158-159; Fadhil and Jiménez 2019, 167 and 169), and in epic (e.g., the epic of Zimrī-Līm, ll. 1-14, see Guichard 2014, 12-24; I am grateful to J. Bach for drawing my attention to this passage).

[54] Metcalf 2015, 37-38.

[55] The lack of narrative portions is a typical trait of both Sumerian and Akkadian hymns. However, the Old Babylonian *Agušaya Hymns A-B* and the *Hymn to Adad* include long mythological passages. On this see Metcalf 2015, 63. For the narrative elements of Greek hymns, see Richardson 2015.

the poet expresses their intention to praise the deity. In this formula, numerous verbs meaning "to praise", "to extol", "to sing", are used.[56]

The Hymn to Šamaš adheres only partially to this format. It begins with an invocation to the god, also using the rhetorical device of the *a-a'* structure (ll. 1-4), followed by a description of the god's solar nature. The section following the invocation, however, does not simply list the prerogatives and qualities of Šamaš, as is typical of the *laudes* section, but rather includes a detailed description of his daily journey. This element is not unusual in compositions dedicated to the Sun God[57], whereas the following section that forms the central body of the hymn introduces an unexpected element.

This following section is neither a true narrative (as in the hymns to Agušaya, for example), nor does the author further develop the *laudes* or move on to the *preces*. Instead, the text shifts its tone from hymnic to that of Wisdom Literature[58]: the central part of the text includes a long section devoted to the role of Šamaš as judge. This section unfolds by listing various just and unjust behaviors, which are rewarded or punished by the Sun God. Various figures are mentioned, who may act honestly or dishonestly (e.g., merchants, judges, money lenders, etc.). The style also moves away from the lyrical and imagery-rich style typical of hymns, to a form that suddenly appears closer to prose, while also showing inconsistencies at the metrical level.

Gradually, the text seems to circle back on itself, ending with a second description of Šamaš's daily journey, which mentions his divine qualities and his role as the Sun God, until the conclusion, when the god rests at the end of the day. The final verse (l. 200) may be considered a form of *salutatio*.[59]

As noted above, the *Great Hymn to Šamaš* exhibits a ring structure. It could indeed be argued that all hymns inherently exhibit a ring composition, since there is often a certain similarity between the beginning of a hymn, where the god is invoked and his qualities are praised, and its end, where the deity can, for example, be praised once again (cf., for example, the za-mi$_3$-doxology), or thanked, because they granted grace and long life to the king.[60]

In the case of the *Great Hymn to Šamaš*, the ring structure is achieved through a clear poetic device, namely the description of the sun's daily cycle. This cycle is described from the sun's rising above the mountains, to its spreading over the earth

[56] Such as *nadûm*, *zamārum*, etc. The "Let me praise"-formula is attested in Sumerian hymns, though occurs more often, and in an expanded manner, in the Akkadian tradition. See Metcalf 2015, 62.

[57] Baragli 2022b, 325.

[58] On the definition of Wisdom Literature as a genre, see Beaulieu 2022; for a recent treatment of Mesopotamian Wisdom as a whole, with description of Mesopotamian wisdom texts, their themes and traditions, see Cohen and Wasserman 2021.

[59] However, the use of such an element is otherwise mainly attested in Akkadian hymns from the early first millennium texts (Metcalf 2015, 73).

[60] The closing section of both Sumerian and Akkadian hymns (*preces*) can also take another form, that is, the request to grant the king well-being. See Metcalf 2015, 71-72.

and among men, and then the same elements are again mentioned in reverse order, before the sun returns to its bedchamber.[61]

The Sections of the Šamaš Hymn

It is possible to divide the *Great Hymn to Šamaš* into a number of macro- and micro-sections. The macro-sections can be identified as follows: **1)** hymnic introduction (first part: invocation ll. 1-4; second part, the Sun God's journey: ll. 5-55) **2)** wisdom section (first part, the Sun God interacts with the people: ll. 55-82; second part, the Sun God's divine justice: ll. 83-127) **3)** hymnic conclusion (first part: Šamaš as protector of the weak, ll. 128-155; second part, Šamaš helps those who praise him: ll. 156-173; third part, hymnic close: 174-200).[62]

The hymnic introduction consists of the initial invocation (ll. 1-4) and the description of the divine journey (ll. 5-53). In this portion of the text, Šamaš rises over the mountains and spreads his light over the earth. Note that the opening lines find an echo in ll. 17-20, where the same image seems to be reiterated, i.e., the rising of Šamaš and the gradual spreading of his rays. L.17 indeed once again opens with the participle *mušnammir* (as in ll. 1 and 3), and appears to amplify the description of the sun's light slowly making its way from the sky over the mountains and valleys, repeating elements already mentioned (the sky, the earth, and the mountains) while introducing new ones (the clouds, the grain fields, the peoples of all lands under Šamaš's protection). In ll. 27-30, this image is repeated yet again through an enumeration that quickens the poem's rhythm, adding another new element, the sea: *mīl tâmti ḫursānī erṣeta šamāmī*, "High seas, mountains, earth, and sky" (l. 29). The mention of the sky at the end of the enumeration suggests the cyclical nature of the Sun God's journey, as Šamaš returns to the heavens to recommence his daily cycle. These repetitions not only amplify the opening lines, but also foreshadow the ring structure of the entire composition.

In l. 53, the point of view seems to shift, and we move from the description of the sun to the human dimension:

ll. 53-55:
[*ana*] *mākalti bārûti ana rikis erēni*
[*ana*?] *mušemmî šāʾili pāšir šunāti*
[…] … *ša riksāti kitmusū maḫarka*

[At] the diviner's bowl, at the knotted sprigs of cedar,
[At] the roasting pot (of offerings set out) by the dream interpreter,
who explains visions of the night,
[*Those who are preparing for*] rites kneel before you.

[61] Castellino 1975, 384.

[62] My division into sections follows, to a certain extent, the thematic division proposed by Castellino (1976), although Castellino's is more detailed. For example, my wisdom section overlaps with Castellino's final portion of Section III (83-94) and Section IV (95-129). It is also partially aligned with Reiner's Section III (ll. 99-125; see Reiner 1985, 75).

At this point, the initial macro-section is coming to a close, making way for the next macro-section, characterized by the presence of wisdom tones. As Reiner observes (1985, 74), at this point in the text the focus is on the activities of men and the role that Šamaš plays in relation to them. Following the initial mention of Šamaš's role in divinatory practices (ll. 53-55), we can identify a section in which the theme of the Sun God's justice is introduced (ll. 58-64). This is followed by a description of Šamaš's merciful aspect as protector of travelers, the weak and prisoners, which extends up to l. 82.

In l. 83 the wisdom section opens, and the motif of Šamaš as a judge is further deepened. The "wisdom" macro-section is most fully developed at this point, in the middle part of the composition (ll. 83-127), which includes a list of honest and dishonest behaviors. Those who do not behave ethically, such as the fraudulent merchant, the unjust judge, and the greedy creditor, are punished by the Sun God, and afflicted with bad luck in business, abandonment by family members, and even premature death. Honest behavior, on the other hand, is always rewarded because it "pleases Šamaš" (ll. 100, 106, 119).

At l. 127, the wisdom section closes and the text now approaches its conclusion (third macro-section, "Hymnic conclusion", 128-200): ll. 128-155 form the first part of this section. Here the motif of Šamaš as the protector of the weak is emphasized once again. Between ll. 156-200, the themes introduced at the beginning of the hymn are repeated, with one variation, in that libations, offerings, and prayers to the Sun God are mentioned.[63]

In this last section, after ca. 20 lines, which echo the opening section and present a series of figures all devoted to Šamaš (both human and inhuman, such as the Lahmu-monsters, and even the "locusts of the sea", ll. 171-172), in l. 174 two rhetorical questions ease the transition from one micro-section to another and focus the attention of the reader or listener on the conclusion of the hymn. The final portion of the *Great Hymn to Šamaš* (ll. 174-200) revisits the themes presented at the beginning, emphasizing Šamaš's role as illuminator, regulator of the seasons (e.g., ll. 178-181), and solar deity.

As noted by Reiner (1985, 69-84), each section displays different types of verbal forms. In the hymnic parts (see especially the first 24 lines of the hymn), which focus on Šamaš's role as a solar deity, there is a predominance of participle

[63] The mention of offerings and libations is not unusual in Akkadian hymns and prayers. Akkadian prayers often include references to the so-called "Tun des Beters" (Mayer 1976, 36-37), which is the description of the performative act or ritual that accompanies the prayer. This can be more or less concrete, indicating either specific ritual instructions or simply a general mention of gifts accompanying the prayer. Akkadian hymns, on the other hand, may mention festive celebrations and ceremonies during which the hymn is recited (see, for example, the *Agušaya Hymn* B, v ll. 10-20; cf. Pohl 2022, 10). However, it is difficult to determine how much these references indicate a real *Sitz im Leben* – whether they reflect an actual use of the text as it has come down to us, or if they are purely fictitious and serve a poetic purpose. In the Hymn to Šamaš, the references to the festival are so general that they seem purely literary. Notably, descriptions of fictitious festivals and celebrations are also found in some Greek hymns, e.g. Callimachus' hymn to Demeter, whose cult location is probably imaginary, see Faulkner and Hodkinson 2015, 10.

forms and verbal adjectives. Conversely, the central section, dedicated to human activities, is dominated by verbs in the present tense, although a few nominal forms are also attested. Moreover, when the subject is Šamaš, the hymn employs mostly finite verbal forms in the second person singular (*Du-Stil*[64]); on the other hand, when referring to mankind, third person singular finite verbs are often used (see for example the repetition of *imaḫḫarka* between lines 134-144).

The use of different predicate forms in each section is intentional, aligning with the meaning of each part of the text and reflecting the themes addressed. Indeed, the language used in the hymnic frame of the text aims to convey the infinity and eternity of the god through non-finite verbal forms, a typical feature of Akkadian hymns.[65] A similar sense of timelessness is expressed in the wisdom section, where, however, the text adopts a gnomic tone, using a combination of durative verbs and statives (and very rarely preterite forms).[66] The interplay between nominal and verbal forms is accompanied by alternating the second and third person. As Reiner rightly points out in her study (1985, *passim*), this alternation also reveals the focus of each section: whether it is more concerned with the figure of Šamaš (second person) or with humanity (third person).

Themes, Literary Motifs, and Wisdom

Overall, the text displays literary topoi and themes which are commonly found in compositions dedicated to Šamaš, in both the Sumerian and Akkadian traditions: Šamaš illuminating the world, Šamaš as merciful protector, and Šamaš as judge. The theme of Šamaš traversing the underworld is also mentioned in passing (see at l. 136 the reference to the *Kūbu* demons and the *Anunnaki*).[67] The image of the Sun God reaching the depth of the ocean (ll. 37-38) is also found in some Old Babylonian Sumerian compositions[68], as is the mention of Šamaš as the patron god of merchants.[69]

---

[64] On this kind of technique, and on the *Du-Stil* and *Er-Stil*, see Norden 1956, 143-166.

[65] Metcalf 2015, 63; cf. Metzler 2002, 719-758.

[66] This verb usage is commonly employed to express events in a timeless dimension (Mayer 2002, 381).

[67] For the typical themes in compositions to the Sun God, see Krebernik 2009-2011, 599-600; cf. Baragli 2022a, 92-120.

[68] Cf. Peterson and Baragli 2024, 9; cf. also Metcalf and Ludwig 2017, 7, 9 and 14, see also *infra* the commentary to l. 37.

[69] See Peterson and Baragli (2024, 13-14) for examples on the theme of the Sun God as patron of merchants in some Sumerian literary texts. Furthermore, Peterson and Baragli argue that the very presence of this theme lends support to Lambert's hypothesis that the composition of our hymn could date from the Old Babylonian period (see *infra*: *Vocabulary*). In particular, Peterson and Baragli note that the theme of traveling merchants, along with the exclusive focus on Šamaš in the hymn (unlike other poems where the Sun God appears alongside other deities, such as Inanna) connects this text to other compositions dedicated to Šamaš from Sippar (Peterson and Baragli 2024, 6). This suggests that the Great Šamaš Hymn may also come from Sippar. In this respect, it is worth noting the prominent social roles of merchants and judges in Old Babylonian Sippar, figures deeply involved in the city's trade and economy, who are featured prominently

However, some themes which are common in the Sumerian tradition, especially in ritual prayers, are missing. For example, there is no reference to Šamaš as the protector of widows and orphans, as can be observed in some Kiutu prayers.[70] More remarkably, there is no mention of his chariot.

The depiction of the Sun God's chariot, sometimes accompanied by descriptions of the horses or even mentions of their food, has a ritual function, being typical of Kiutu incantation-prayers especially from the Old and Middle Babylonian periods.[71] This motif is associated with the moment when a Kiutu prayer was recited as part of a ritual, specifically between dawn and sunrise.[72] Occasionally, the theme of the chariot is not mentioned directly in Kiutu texts, but other elements, which indirectly point to it (e.g., the bridle or the charioteer), are present.[73]

The complete absence of the chariot motif in the Šamaš Hymn is significant and contributes to our understanding of its context and use. Unlike Kiutu prayers, which typically focus on specific parts of the sun's journey (e.g., sunrise or sunset), the Šamaš Hymn describes the sun's journey in its entirety.[74] This broader perspective supports the idea that the hymn was likely not intended for ritual use. Strengthening this hypothesis are two key points: the hymn is never referenced in any ritual instructions, and there are no elements in any of the manuscripts of the text that suggest it had a ritual purpose (i.e., a subscript or rubric). This might explain why the chariot motif is absent from the hymn.

The depiction of the Sun God's movement as a cyclic phenomenon, not tied to a specific time of day, is also found in a bilingual Hymn to Utu.[75] This text is considered by some to be a forerunner of our Great Hymn. However, while Sumerian hymns to Utu[76] – or at least some of them, as confirmed by their rubrics[77] – were probably recited as part of the cultic liturgy in temples, there is no evidence

in our hymn. This reinforces the idea that the hymn may indeed have originated in Sippar during the Old Babylonian period. On role of merchants and judges in Old Babylonian Sippar, see Harris 1975, cf. De Graef 2014, in particular 213-216. See also De Graef's remark (ibid., 212): "The titles and patronyms of the creditors show that the palace wool trade in Sippar was mainly in the hands of judges and merchants [...].". Cf. also Kalla 2009-2011, 530, with further references. For more on the commercial activities in Sippar, see Veenhof 2004 with previous literature; on merchants in third millennium Mesopotamia, see Garfinkle 2010.

[70] For the theme of the Sun God protecting widows and orphans (among other categories of people in need) in Kiutu prayers see Baragli 2022a, 112-113.

[71] Baragli 2022a, 76-77. The motif of the chariot declines in its use in first millennium sources.

[72] The Kiutu prayers are recited at significant religious and ritual times, specifically at "liminal" times of the day, such as sunrise or sunset (Baragli 2022a, 49). The description of the sun's chariot was probably recited at sunrise, and highlights the moment when Šamaš begins his journey, while the descriptions of food preparation and the bridle mirror actual ritual practice. Baragli 2022a, 49-50: "Während auf einer rituellen Ebene das Futter und das Zaumzeug für die Pferde des Sonnenwagens vorbereitet werden, beginnt auf einer mythischen Ebene der Sonnenwagen seine Reise." See also Alaura and Bonechi 2012, 12.

[73] Baragli 2022a, 77.

[74] Baragli 2022b, 326.

[75] Baragli 2022b, 325-326.

[76] Alster and Jeyes 1990, 8; cf. Baragli 2022b, 325.

[77] Baragli 2022b, 322.

that the Hymn to Šamaš was used in this way (although a cultic setting of some sort cannot be excluded).

While one would not normally expect wisdom themes and topoi to appear in hymns, some of those which appear here – such as the reference to dishonest merchants (see, e.g., the fragmentary hymns to Šamaš from Ugarit[78]) – are often found in other hymns and prayers to the Sun (God). A parallel to the motif of the dishonest merchant is also found in two Hittite prayers, as noted by Reiner in her study of the present text.[79]

Elements in the Šamaš hymn that most closely resemble Wisdom Literature, simultaneously diverging from the standard language of religious poetry, are parallels to wisdom texts, such as the *Counsels of Wisdom* and *Ludlul*. A formulation occurring in two lines of the former closely parallels three lines of the Šamaš hymn.[80] Another parallel, albeit a weaker one which might simply be regarded as a similar formulation, occurs at l. 117 of the Šamaš Hymn and *Ludlul* I, l. 62.[81] In addition, certain formulas and expressions from the Hymn to Šamaš recur in a similar way in another wisdom text, *Šimâ milka*. For example, lines 88 and 115 of this hymn echo similar thoughts and phrases found in lines 27 and 25 of *Šimâ milka*.[82]

The existence of parallels between our text and other texts does not necessarily indicate a direct intertextual relationship. This is to say that there is no evidence of a specific dependence of our hymn on these compositions, or vice versa. Considering the universal tone of the aforementioned parallels, it seems plausible to suggest that they are literary echoes, wisdom formulas that were well-known and reused across different texts. However, the verses 98-119 of our hymn, which form the core of the wisdom section, are homogeneous in content and style and are also

[78] Cf. e.g. l. 9 (rev.) of The Hymn to Šamaš RS 20.231(+) RS 25.443, where the line, though fragmentary, reads: [giš]*zi-ba-ni-it sa-ar-ti*[!], "The dishonest weighing scales", in Arnaud 2007, 109. Arnaud further remarks: "Le thème de la balance fausse est banal dans les hymnes à Šamaš" (2007, 109).

[79] See Reiner 1985, 77; the Hittite prayers showing the parallel are CTH 372 and CTH 374 (edited by Schwemer 2015 and more recently by Rieken et al. 2017; see supra fn. 31). The comparable passages are found in CTH 372, ll. 150-153: "'[I, a mor]tal, what have I do[ne] t[o my god? The merchant man holds] the s[cales] towards [the Su]n-god [and] falsi[fies the sc]ales (nevertheless).'" (Schwemer 2015, 382; 388); and in CTH 374, ll. 62″-64″: "The merchant man holds the scales towards the Sun-god and falsifies the scales (nevertheless). But I, what have I done (to you,) my God?" (Schwemer 2015, 367, 371).

[80] E.g., *Counsels of Wisdom* ll. A+11; A+15 (Földi 2022a): *ṭāb eli Šamaš irâbšu dumqa*, "It is pleasing to Šamaš, he will requite him with favor", paralleling ll. 100, 106 and 119 of the Šamaš Hymn.

[81] See Ludlul I, l. 62 in Hätinen 2022: *errub bītuššu rebû itamma*, "'I'll take over his household!', vows the fourth."

[82] L. 25 of *Šimâ milka* runs as follows: *tarašši bilta biltu ḫarruptu*, "you will acquire a yield: a premature burden" (my translation), featuring the similar use of *rašû* with *biltu*, as in our text. Regarding this parallel between *Šimâ milka* and the Šamaš Hymn, and the difficulties in translating l. 25 of *Šimâ milka*, cf. the discussion in de Zorzi 2019 with previous references; l. 27 of *Šimâ milka* has: *e tešši īnīka ana aššat amēli*, "Don't covet another man's wife", the same concept expressed in the Šamaš Hymn, l. 88. For the latest edition of *Šimâ milka*, see Cohen 2013.

characterized by commercial terms and expressions that contrast with the rest of the composition (see *infra*: *Vocabulary*). This homogeneity suggests that they may originate from a specific wisdom text. Nevertheless, it is not possible to trace them back to a precise source (or, we could say, to a definite hypotext).[83] They could, for instance, belong to a series of proverbs, although this is impossible to verify, and the wisdom composition from which these verses may have been taken remains a "ghost" composition for the time being.[84]

The parallels with *Ludlul*, *Counsels of Wisdom,* and other expressions borrowed from texts of different literary genres (such as other hymns and prayers, or the series *Šurpu*[85]) contribute to the diverse styles within the Hymn to Šamaš, leading to a central section that exhibits a different manner compared to the beginning and the end of the composition.

The concept of wisdom underlying the central section represents so-called "positive" wisdom. Based on the *Tun-Ergehen* mechanism,[86] this notion of divine justice is the most common in Mesopotamian wisdom and religion, asserting that good deeds are rewarded and bad deeds are punished. This contrasts with so-called 'negative' wisdom, which implies a more critical approach to religion.[87]

Narrative Strategies: Space and Focalization

Space plays a very important role in the Hymn to Šamaš. Within the hymnic framework of the text, the places where the god acts during his daily journey are mentioned: the sky, the mountains, the earth, the ocean, and the underworld. These are not elaborate descriptions, but rather an enumeration, in which the names are

[83] On the problem of identifying an unknown hypotext with regard to Akkadian literary texts, and intertextuality in general as applied to Akkadian literature, see Jiménez 2017a, 80-82.

[84] On this see Nakata's remarks (1970, 93): "The refrain (line 100), [...] suggests that at least lines 99-100 were taken from a group, if not a collection, of didactic sayings which had existed prior to the composition of the present Shamash hymn." The practice of reworking and reusing wisdom texts in other texts is well documented in Mesopotamian literature. For instance, proverbs were occasionally reused, even shortened to the point that they became difficult to comprehend, see for example Cohen 2013, 83 and 106; cf. Alster 2007, 5-6, and note also Alster 2007, 6-7 on another practice, that is, proverbs quoting literary texts. Compare the similar phenomenon in the Akkadian Disputation Poems, which occasionally quote the Theodicy, see Jiménez 2017a, 89. Note that, within the present hymn, it is possible to find another example of a truncated stock-phrase in l. 125: "The nay-sayers' testimonies are before you", see on this the commentary on the line in Lambert 1960a, 322.

[85] For the intertextual parallels with other texts, see Lambert 1960a, 123. Cf. also the possible allusion to the Šamaš Hymn in the "*Dialogue of Pessimism*", ll. 62-69 (// ll. 118-121 of the present hymn) and ll. 71-73 (// ll. 122-123), see Hurowitz 2007.

[86] For a brief summary of the definition of *Tun-Ergehen-Zusammenhang*, see Oshima 2018, 189-190, with previous literature.

[87] On "positive" and "negative" wisdom see Cohen 2013, 14-15. "Negative" wisdom, according to Cohen, employs two interrelated concepts: 1) nothing has value, 2) therefore one should enjoy life as much as possible ("Vanity theme"; see Cohen 2013, 15). In Akkadian literature, a similar critical thinking can be found, e.g., in *Ludlul* or the *Babylonian Theodicy*, both of which address the question of divine justice and offer reflections on the inevitable suffering of human life.

occasionally characterized by adjectives (e.g., "distant mountains", l. 6, the "vast earth", l. 28 etc.).

The space where men are subjected to the judgment of Šamaš is also not described in detail, instead being only hinted at through the mention of a few generic places (the rough sea where seafarers sail, the roads shown to prisoners, the prisons from which prisoners are rescued, the underworld, etc.; see ll. 66-75).

Space is thus illustrated in the text concisely. The manner is almost cinematic, as individual images help to create a general picture in the mind of the reader or listener. The description follows the movement of the Sun as he travels through the hemispheres.

As convincingly shown by Reiner, the narrative not only follows Šamaš on his journey, but also zooms in on various aspects. From the vast spaces traversed by the sun, the text shifts to human activities: the roads traveled by wayfarers, the dangerous sea, the prisons into which prisoners are cast. Interestingly, the narrative perspective is that of the god himself: it is through the eyes of Šamaš that we observe the mountains he traverses and the world below, gradually focusing on human actions.[88]

This can be described as a "panoramic" focus, one that is distanced from the scene being described. More specifically, it is an "*actorial* panoramic standpoint". According to de Jong's definition, this narrative technique involves the narrator adopting the perspective of one of the characters – in this case, the god Šamaš.[89]

[88] Through her analysis of the verbal forms used in the text, Reiner (1985, 68-84; see supra) has shown how the hymn is characterized by a great narrative dynamism, with continuous zooming in and out of different scenes. For a comparable narrative strategy, see also the bird's-eye view found in *Etana*, as the hero and the eagle ascend to heaven (Horowitz 1990, 515-516); cf. also Wasserman 2020, 142 for a description of a similar narrative strategy in the epic of *Atraḫasīs*.

[89] It is important to stress that the narrator is never Šamaš himself; rather, it is the poet (or, we could say, the author) who, at this point of the hymn, assumes the god's point of view. The sun god functions as the divine addressee, as it is typical of hymns and clearly illustrated in this text by the use of verbs in second person and the pronominal suffix *-ka*, as well as the appeal found at l. 148. As the composition progresses, the bird's-eye viewpoint shifts to reflect the perspective of the people under Šamaš's influence (see *infra*). Therefore, we can also describe the narrative mode of the *Hymn to Šamaš* as comparable to what Genette terms "internal focalization," where the narrator conveys only what the character knows (cf. Genette 1988, 65-66; for more on focalization and narratology techniques, see *The Living Handbook of Narratology by* P. Hühn *et al.* http://www.lhn.uni-hamburg.de/. 2013, last accessed 09.23.2024). For the "panoramic perspective", and for a general narratological analysis of space in ancient hymns, see de Jong 2012, 39-55, who examines the Homeric Hymns. Similar considerations to those made by de Jong are also relevant for Akkadian hymns. Incidentally, the same zooming mechanism and panoramic/cinematic perspective have been observed by Umberto Eco in the opening of a much later text, "The Betrothed" (*I Promessi Sposi*) by Alessandro Manzoni. The description Eco gives of the first lines of the Italian novel could easily be applied to the Hymn to Šamaš: "Manzoni ha deciso che la sua descrizione dell'ambiente deve procedere anzitutto per un movimento che un tecnico cinematografico chiamerebbe di "zoom", è come se la ripresa fosse fatta da un aereo: cioè la descrizione parte come fatta dagli occhi di Dio, non dagli occhi degli abitanti. Questa prima opposizione 'alto verso basso', [...], individua prima il lago e il suo ramo, poi scende lentamente a guardare il ponte e le rive. [...] La visione geografica, man mano che procede dall'alto verso il basso, diventa visione topografica e include potenzialmente gli osservatori umani." (published in the magazine *L'Espresso*, 24.02.1985).

Linked to this panoramic focus is an omnitemporal narrative, expressed mainly through participles and stative verbs, which refers to an ever-present reality, suspended in time: the natural phenomenon of the sun rising and setting every day.[90]

The change that occurs in verse 54 is noteworthy, with the abrupt mention of the diviner's bowl and the roasting pot (this technique is called "close-up standpoint"[91]). At this juncture, the narrator effectuates a change in the description, zooming in on the human characters. This coincides with a modification in the language, since the second-person singular form is progressively mixed with the third-person singular and plural (as evidenced by the later repetition of *imaḫḫarka*). In l. 148, the text reaches its climax with a sudden invocation of the deity in the first person. This appeal – a direct plea to the Šamaš not to forsake the different categories of people mentioned earlier – serves as a transition point. It signifies the end of the detailed descriptions or "vignettes"[92] of the human world. Gradually, the focus moves away from the human realm and back to the divine. It is therefore possible to identify three levels of description in our text: the distant lands, mountains and seas; the places inhabited by the people caught up in their daily activities; and the objects. The perspective never shifts: everything remains under the ever-watching eye of Šamaš.[93]

Original Composition or Pastiche?

The overall inhomogeneity of the hymn to Šamaš, which appears to be composed of disparate textual units that vary in tone and content, was already observed by Lambert in his edition of the text. Due to the hymn's uneven structure, Lambert proposed that the text was a "patchwork" composition. That is, it was composed in various stages, perhaps starting from an original kernel, into which later portions were gradually incorporated.[94]

---

[90] On omnitemporal narrative, see de Jong 2014, 100-101. Cf. Baragli 2023, 201 and 204, who observed the same technique in the Kiutu prayers.

[91] See De Jong 2012, XI, for the definition of "close-up" in narratology, cf. also ibid. 13 for an example.

[92] Reiner 1985, 77.

[93] Cf. the similar remarks of Akujärvi (2012, 241) in reference to a description in Pausanias's *Periegesis*.

[94] Lambert 1960a, 124. Lambert also suggests two other possibilities: either that the text is the result of a late reworking of an older text, or that it is a late original composition based on older material. However, the hypothesis of a text composed by incorporating lines, stanzas, or even entire portions borrowed from different texts is more likely. This practice finds correspondence both in the Akkadian tradition (cf. *Hymn to the Queen of Nippur*, last edited by Földi 2021b, or, for example, a late syncretistic hymn to Marduk, *Eriš šummi*, edited recently by Fadhil and Jiménez 2022) and in the Sumerian tradition (see Delnero 2020, 137-138, on a similar practice occurring in the composition of Balaĝs, which often show the repetition of same lines or textual blocks, i.e., "Versatzstücke"). See also the composition of group CTH 372-374, cited above, which probably involved the combination of multiple Sumerian and Akkadian textual materials (Schwemer forthcoming).

Further indication of a text-building process, which took place in several stages, is the material form of many of the Šamaš Hymn manuscripts. As previously observed, the most distinctive physical feature of the manuscripts of this hymn, as well as other manuscripts of the "Great Hymns and Prayers," is the division into couplets, achieved by the addition of horizontal rulings on the tablets every two verses.

This division is intrinsically linked to the poetic device *par excellence* of Akkadian poetry – parallelism – which is extensively used in the text under consideration (see *infra*). However, the horizontal rulings are not always applied consistently within our text. As noted by Lambert, there is not always a precise correspondence between the couplets of the hymn and the graphic division on the tablet. Indeed, in some cases, one can observe groups of three verses instead of two, or couplets that, although logically connected, are separated by ruling.[95]

The inconsistency in the use of rulings supports the hypothesis that the text was composed in multiple stages. It is likely that new verses were gradually added, disrupting the original order and overall structure of the text. Such a phenomenon can be also observed in Marduk 1, when one compares the Old Babylonian version of the text with the manuscripts that have survived from the first millennium.[96] An Old Babylonian manuscript of the Šamaš Hymn is as yet unattested, so it is uncertain whether a forerunner of the text exhibited a consistent division into couplets. Nevertheless, the features mentioned thus far, such as style inconsistencies and material aspect, suggest a process similar to that which occurred in Marduk 1.

Despite its irregularity, the couplet division of the present hymn was clearly considered important by Akkadian scribes. In fact, the Šamaš Hymn was probably understood to be composed of couplets, as evidenced not only by the library manuscripts, which show horizontal rulings, but also by a school manuscript from Assur (VAT 10174, here AššNASch1). In this manuscript, which preserves lines 143-154 of the Šamaš Hymn, each line contains two lines of our text, divided by a division mark (i.e., a Glossenkeil).[97] This indicates that the text was learned in a distich format, suggesting that scribes were already familiar with this textual structure during their training.

Another hymn belonging to the corpus of the so-called Great hymns and prayers, namely the hymn to Ištar Queen of Nippur, displays a form that is comparable to that of the Hymn to Šamaš and appears to be similarly composite in nature. This hymn is also composed of a series of textual units that are distinct from

---

[95] Lambert 1960a, 123; cf. Reiner 1985, 69.

[96] Although the Old Babylonian manuscript of Marduk 1 (BM 78728, CT 44, 21) is only partially preserved, it seems to respect the division of the text into couplets: the manuscript seems to be structured into pairs of distichs, being divided through a horizontal line every four verses. This division is disrupted in later manuscripts, likely due to the insertion of "filler lines". On this see Fadhil and Jiménez 2019, 162 and Rozzi 2024b, 336-337.

[97] See Maul and Manasterska 2023 (*KAL* 15), Nr. 33; cf. Rozzi 2021a. For a more detailed discussion of the division into couplets of the manuscripts of the Šamaš Hymn, see Rozzi 2024b, 333-34.

one another. It appears to be the result of a literary pastiche,[98] in which parts of different texts were borrowed to create the text that has survived to the present day.[99]

However, in contrast to the hymn to Ištar Queen of Nippur, whose textual sections are so disparate in terms of language, tone, and content that they appear to lack overall cohesion, the hymn to Šamaš, in its extant form, exhibits a certain unity. This is despite the quotations from different texts and genres, the variable style, and even the inconsistencies in the material features of its manuscripts.

Manuscript Tradition

The Šamaš Hymn is preserved on forty manuscripts, 22 of which are school exercise tablets[100]. Three Babylonian sources are commentaries (BabLBQuo1, BabLBQuo2, SipNBQuo1). All the manuscripts can be dated to the first millennium, one from Babylon even dating to the first century BCE. Most of the manuscripts are in Babylonian script, while 15 are written in Assyrian script. As can be seen from the Table of Manuscripts (see *infra*), 6 manuscripts come from Nineveh, 21 from Babylon or Babylonia, 8 from Sippar and 4 from Assur. In addition, one manuscript from Uruk was recently identified.[101]

The wide-spread dissemination of this text and the abundance of copies on school tablets suggest that the Šamaš Hymn was considered a "literary classic", such as other famous texts like Marduk 1 and *Ludlul*.[102] Moreover, the text is quoted in three commentaries, which further proves its popularity.

The Assyrian manuscripts are all datable to the seventh century BCE. The manuscripts from Nineveh probably come from the Southwest Palace.[103] They are written in the typical 8th-7th century Neo-Assyrian script and all of them display the division of the text into couplets by horizontal rulings. All the Nineveh manuscripts are two-column tablets, two of which preserve a colophon (type f, no. 320 in Hunger 1986).

---

[98] I use the term "pastiche" here in a broad sense, drawing on Fadhil and Jiménez 2022, 256-257, to refer to a text which imitates another composition or borrows passages from it.

[99] Lambert 1982, 178.

[100] For photos of these manuscripts and further information (e.g., further relevant publications), see the section "List of Manuscripts" in the online edition on the eBL platform (https://www.ebl.lmu.de/corpus/L/3/4, last accessed 08.08.2024). Cf. also Rozzi 2024a. For the sake of clarity, I have kept the same names of the manuscripts in the online edition. Several of these manuscripts were identified during the course of the eBL project and edited by the present author (Rozzi 2021b, Rozzi 2022b, Rozzi 2023).

[101] Identification by T. Mitto.

[102] On other "Literary classics" in Babylonian literature, see Fadhil and Jiménez 2019.

[103] Most of the tablets from the Kuyunjik (K) and Sm collections probably come from the Southwest palace. See Reade 2000, 422, and George 2003, 385.

Of the four Assyrian manuscripts found in Assur, three are school exercise tablets: AššNASch1 (VAT 10174), AššNASch2 (VAT 100171) and AššNASch3 (VAT 10756). The precise findspot of AššNASch1 is unknown, whereas AššNASch2 comes from the so-called "House of the Scribes" (N2).[104] Despite the fact that the textual quotations in AššNASch3 come from the same sources as those in AššNASch2, and even precede them immediately in the original texts from which they are extracted, the findspot of AššNASch3 is probably not the same of AššNASch2 and remains uncertain.[105] The Assur school tablets AššNASch2 and AššNASch3 are typical examples of the type 2a school tablets, showing extracts from incantations, literary texts, and lexical lists.[106] AššNASch1 represents a unique case among the school tablets found in Assur, as it includes, alongside the excerpt from the Šamaš Hymn, other long literary excerpts from similarly complex compositions (e.g., "A Hymn in Praise of Babylon and the Babylonians," Marduk 2, and the *Epic of Erra*, see above fn. 43). It is the only known school tablet from Assur known so far that contains exclusively literary excerpts.[107] This tablet is comparable to the type of school tablets from Nippur defined as "2d" by E. Jiménez, which consist of unusually long tablets with a higher-than-average number of excerpts.[108] AššNASch1 was likely an exercise intended for more advanced students.

The Babylonian manuscripts represent a more diverse range of sources, since they can be dated from the Neo-Babylonian period to the first century BCE.

Among the manuscripts stemming from Sippar, three probably come from Rassam's excavation in Abu Habba (SipNB4a, to be joined with SipNB4b; SipNBSch1 and SipNBSch3)[109], while SipNB3a (Si. 15) comes from Scheil's excavations and was erroneously described by Scheil as a bilingual fragment ("Fragment d'un texte religieux bilingue", Scheil 1902, 103). To SipNB3a could (indirectly) join two more fragments, SipNB3b and SipNB3c.[110] Their exact findspot is unknown. The Sippar tablet SipNB1 (IM 124633), edited by George and Al-Rawi (1998), comes from the Niche 2B of the Sippar library (see George and Al-Rawi 1998, 201). The majority of the manuscripts from Babylon or Borsippa come from the excavations of Rassam (BabNB1, BabNB2, BabLBSch1, BabLBSch4, BabLBSch5, BabLBSch6, BabLBSch7, BabLBSch10, BabLBSch14, BabLBSch15, BabLBQuo1), while others were purchased from dealers (e.g., BabLBSch3, BabLBSch8, BabLBSch9 belonging to the Spartali collection). One manuscript was excavated by Koldewey at Babylon (George and Taniguchi 2019, no. 142).

---

[104] That is, a house close to the ziggurat of Assur where a scribal family used to live. See Pedersén, ALA 2, 29-34; Maul and Manasterska 2023, 27.

[105] See Maul and Manasterska 2023, 51.

[106] Gesche 2000, 174.

[107] See Maul and Manasterska 2023, 115.

[108] Jiménez 2022, 29, 257-258.

[109] Judging from their registration numbers: 82-9-18 (SipNB4a, SipNB4b, SipNBSch1) and 82-5-22 (SipNBSch2 and SipNBSch3), see Leichty 1986; Leichty and Grayson 1987.

[110] The indirect join was proposed within the eBL project by E. Jiménez.

A significant number of the Babylonian manuscripts are school tablets, and one of them, from Babylon, merits particular attention, as it belongs to the corpus of the so-called Graeco-Babyloniaca (BabLBSch2[111]), and probably dates from the first century BCE.[112]

The manuscript UrkLB1 (IM 135964) was found in Uruk and is probably Late Babylonian. However, it is difficult to say for certain as its findspot has been disturbed by later burials.[113]

The manuscripts, both Assyrian and Babylonian, display an overall similarity in spelling conventions. Furthermore, they do not show significant textual variants, except for few cases (e.g., l. 159; see *infra*: *Textual Variants*) and thus often diverge in orthographic features only (e.g. in l. 170 the spelling *šá-di-i* is attested in the Babylonian witnesses preserving the line, while the Niniveh sources have KUR.MEŠ). Often, variants are probably due to scribal errors.

The Assyrian manuscripts tend to respect the practices of Standard Babylonian, although they show the typical features of first millennium orthographic spellings, such as the lack of mimation and occasionally erratic case endings (cf. Streck 2014). In a few cases, Assyrianisms can be observed (e.g., *e-pu-šu* for *īpušū* in NinNA3b iii, 1′, and NinNA4c iv, 8′). The school manuscripts from Assur are generally free of errors, with only a few exceptions.

The Babylonian manuscripts display the standard features of Late Babylonian, as well as late spellings.[114] Contrary to the school manuscripts from Assur, those from Babylonia exhibit numerous errors.

Below are some examples of spelling conventions found in the manuscripts. The manuscripts are differentiated here between Assyrian (A) and Babylonian (B). It is worth noting that the differentiation between Late Babylonian and Neo-Babylonian manuscripts should be approached with caution, as the precise dating of the tablets proves to be difficult in many cases.[115] If, in certain cases, the ductus seems to suggest a Neo-Babylonian dating rather than Late Babylonian, as seen in

[111] According to Geller (1997, 78), the tablet might be part of another tablet (BM 33778).

[112] The dating of the Graeco-Babyloniaca is a matter of debate due to the lack of precise information available. There are no dates in the colophons of the tablets, and the archival context is unclear. Nevertheless, the most probable date is the late second or early first century BCE. For an overview of this corpus with precedent references, see Lang 2023, 130-137.

[113] IM 135964 was found near the *Wannengrab* 298. See Hunger 1972, 79 and 85.

[114] For a description of the typical features of Late Babylonian, see Jiménez 2017a, 225; 276-280; 352-353.

[115] Although a comprehensive treatment of late palaeography is still lacking (the new ERC-funded project RECC led by E. Jiménez at LMU Munich will address this desideratum), valuable insights can be obtained from databases like LaBaSi (https://labasi.acdh.oeaw.ac.at/) or eBL (https://www.ebl.lmu.de/signs). For studies on Late Babylonian epigraphy, see Jursa 2015 and Pirngruber 2019. Cf. also Debourse (2022, 179-181), who offers useful examples of palaeographic differences between certain Hellenistic and Neo-Babylonian sign forms. Another noteworthy study is Arbøll 2023, 72-75, which compares paleographic features in Middle Babylonian and Neo-Babylonian scripts, with further references. For a description of the differences between Neo-Babylonian and Late Babylonian script, see also Fadhil and Jiménez 2024 (§4 The Manuscripts).

SipNB3b or SipNB4a,[116] one should bear in mind that "archaizing" manuscripts, i.e. manuscripts imitating older script forms, was not an uncommon practice in the first millennium.[117]

All manuscripts are further separated into library manuscripts and school tablets (Sch). Logograms, variants and scribal mistakes will be described separately.

The following list is not exhaustive, but serves only to illustrate the general traits observable in the manuscripts that preserve the Hymn to Šamaš.

Writing Conventions and Orthography

In the Nineveh manuscripts, the spelling of nouns in the *status rectus* reflects the typical Neo-Assyrian tendency to merge the nominative and accusative cases, favoring the vowel *-u*.[118] Similarly, due to the general neglect of short final vowels, commonly observed in first-millennium Babylonian sources, numerous variations in case endings also occur in the Babylonian manuscripts of the Šamaš Hymn. The variation in the spelling of case endings is so widespread across the manuscripts under study, that adjacent words, serving identical logical-grammatical functions, occasionally display different final vowels (see e.g. 176 *e-ṭu-tu*$_4$ and *uk-li* in NinaNA1, both genitives in the phrase).[119] As can be seen in the examples below, library manuscripts (L) and school tablets (Sch) often present the same spelling variations.

Nominative nouns in the manuscripts of the Šamaš hymn can take the expected case endings *-u*, *-i*, and, more rarely, *-a*. However, nominatives in *-i* are found in both Assyrian and Babylonian sources, including school fragments:

A (L): 51 *te-ne-še-ti* for *tenēšētu* (NinNA1 and NinNA2b); 118 *um-ma-ni* for *ummânu* (NinNA4c); 137 [*k*]*a-par-ri* for *kaparru* (NinNA1).
(Sch): 138 *a-lak-ti* for *alaktu* (AššNASch2).

---

[116] In these manuscripts certain sign forms suggest a Neo-Babylonian dating. In general, even if drawing hard and fast conclusions is problematic, it can be said that the Late Babylonian form of MEŠ is distinguishable from Neo-Babylonian MEŠ from the oblique wedges, which are traced higher over the horizontal wedge, and appear more strongly inclined diagonally. In addition, signs like KU and LU tend to lose the first horizontal wedge in Late Babylonian writing. In SipNB4a, one can easily identify Neo-Babylonian MEŠ (rev. 16), KU, and LU (obv. 11′ and 13′ respectively). SipNB3b displays a Neo-Babylonian LU in rev. 11. For a discussion on the paleography of these signs, see Jursa 2015; cf. also the remarks in Frame and George 2005, 266 and Fadhil and Jiménez 2024, *Group 2: Late Babylonian Manuscripts*.

[117] Consider, for instance, the *Syncretistic Hymn to Ištar*, the Babylonian manuscript of which is dated to the fourth century BCE but exhibits a script that imitates an earlier style of writing (latest edition by Földi 2021a).

[118] The Neo-Assyrian tendency towards two cases (nominative/accusative in *-u*, and genitive in *-i/e*) is probably a consequence of the Babylonian influence. See Luukko 2004, 189; cf. also Leonhardt 2024, §C.88.

[119] This phenomenon is not rare and also occurs, e.g., in both Assyrian and Babylonian manuscripts of the *Maqlû* series; see Schwemer 2017, 70.

B (L): 118 *um-ma-ni* for *ummânu* (SipNB3a); 138 *ki-ni* for *kīnu* (SipNB3a).
(Sch): 118 *um-ma-ni* for *ummânu* (BabaLBSch12); 118 *ki-i-ni* for *kīnu* (BabaLBSch12).

Nominatives in *-a* are very few and mostly attested in the Assyrian manuscripts:

A (L): 56 *ki-na* for *kīnu* (NinNA1); 101 *da-a-a-na* for *dayānu* (NinNA1); 139 *al-la-ka* for *allāku* (NinNA1).
B (L): 139 *al-la-ka* for *allāku* (SipNB1).

In addition, nouns in accusative show, beside the standard ending *-a*, endings in *-u* and *-i*. The ending in *-u* is far more common, and, as expected, is primarily found in the Neo-Assyrian manuscripts:

A (L): 49 *li-šá-nu* for *lišāna* (NinNA1 and NinNA2b); 68 *ma-ḫi-ru* for *māḫira* (NinNA2a);
96 *ka-pi-du* for *kāpida* (NinNA2b); 98 *muš-te-še-ru* for *muštēšira* (NinNA2b); 131 *su-up-pu-ú su-ul-lu-ú ka-ra-bu* for *suppâ sullâ karāba* (NinNA3b); 150 *šam-ru* for *šamra* (NinNA1).
(Sch): 150 *šam-ru* for *šamra* (AššNASch1).
B (L): 96 *ka-pi-du* for *kāpida* (SipNB4a and SipNB3b); 106 *ba-la-ṭu* for *balāṭa* (SipNB4a); 150 *šam-ri* for *šamra* (SipNB1).
(Sch): 106 *ba-la-ṭu* for *balāṭa* (BabLBSch6).

Accusatives in *-i* are rare, but can be found (in the majority of cases) in the Babylonian manuscripts, especially school tablets:

A (L): 71 *mun-nar-bi* for *munnarba* (NinNA1).
B (L): 97 *ṣal-pi* for *ṣalpa* and *me-se-ri* for *mēsera* (SipNB4a).
(Sch): 70 *kap-pi* for *kap-pa* (BabLBSch1 and BabLBSch3); 71 *mun-nar-bi* for *munnarba* (BabLBSch1).

Genitives also attest a variety of case endings: final *-u* genitives are often found, with genitives in *-a* occurring more rarely:

A (L): 124 *lum-nu* for *lumni* (NinNA1 and NinNA4c); 127 *rug-gu-gu* for *ruggugi* (NinNA1).
B (L): 34 *kiš-šá-ta* for *kiššati* (SipNB3a); 84 *da-mu* for *dāmi* (BabLB and SipNB4a); 98-99 *ṭa-a-tú* for *ṭāti* (SipNB4a); 93 *da-a-a-nu* for *dayāni* in SipNB4a.
(Sch): 6 *bi-ru-tu* for *bērūti* (BabLBSch4); 53 *ba-ru-tú* for *bārûti* (BabLBSch8); 121 *da-ru-ú* for *dārî* (BabLBSch16); 167 *ṣal-pa-*⸢*tu*$_4$⸣ for *ṣalipti* (BabLBSch13).

As is typical of first-millennium manuscripts, mimation is nowhere to be found in any of the sources, but the signs TUM and TIM are used sparsely at the end of nouns. The use of TUM and TIM does not always adhere to the expected end-vowel (e.g., 171 *pu-luḫ*-TUM for *puluḫta* (SipNBSch1); 29 KI-T]IM (NinNA1), KI-TIM (SipNB3a), both for *erṣeta*).[120]

In certain cases, nouns in *status constructus* display an additional vowel (*u* or *i*), making it difficult to ascertain whether this reflects later orthographic conventions or indicates a poetic feature that reproduces an archaic spelling.[121] For Assyrian manuscripts, an archaism is more likely. For Babylonian sources, it might simply reflect the Neo-Babylonian tendency to use overhanging vowels in nouns and verbs.[122] Another typical phenomenon of late Babylonian manuscripts, the syncope of short final vowels, can be observed in one library manuscript from Sippar (SipNB3a) and, noticeably, in one Graeco-Babyloniaca manuscript (BabLBSch2): l. 184 of the hymn, SipNB3a iv 17′: *ba-bi*]*l pa-an* for *bābil pāni*; l. 169-171 of the hymn, BabLBSch2 rev. 1: ⌜ρ?⌝[α]φασθ for *rapašta*, rev. 2 ε]⌜λ⌝ουθ for *elûti*, rev. 3 φολοξθ for *puluḫta*.[123]

The spelling of verbal forms generally adheres to Standard Babylonian. The phenomenon of overhanging vowels in middle-weak verbs is only observable in a few cases (e.g. *ṭāb(i)*, l. 100, 106, 109). The tendency of Late Babylonian to prefer a final vowel *-u* in verbs is attested, for example, in l. 166, where the form *idallalā* is written *i-dal-la-lu* in both Babylonian manuscripts where it is preserved (SipNBSch1, obv. 4′; BabLBSch13, obv. 4′). Note that the same form is attested as ⌜*i-dal*⌝-*lal* in the Nineveh manuscript NinNA2a, iii 8′.

Another example of preferential use of the *-u* vowel is found in BabNB1, obv. 9′, and BabLBSch1, obv. 20′, which write an expected *uṣṣi* (84) as ⌜*uṣ-ṣu*⌝ and ⌜*ú-ṣu*⌝ respectively.[124]

Theme vowels do not exhibit variation in either Babylonian or the Assyrian manuscript tradition. Only one example is attested: 147 *takli*, spelled *tak-la* in SipNB1 (*takālu*). Yet this verb typically exhibits alternation between *a/i*.[125]

[120] See Schwemer 2017, 72-73, for a similar phenomenon in the *Maqlû* manuscripts.

[121] The insertion of an unexpected vowel *-i* in the construct state, which appears as a **parsi*-pattern instead of **paras*, is a feature found in Akkadian literary texts, likely stemming from the construct state in *-i* in Old Akkadian (George 2003, 432; cf. Schwemer 2017, 79). Furthermore, unexpected final vowels in construct chains are a typical characteristic of the so-called "Hymno-Epic Dialect" (see *infra*), particularly used in Akkadian hymns. Old Babylonian hymns commonly exhibit a construct state in *-u* or *-i* in singular nouns, suggesting that these forms should be interpreted as poeticisms (Pohl 2022, 48). Epic texts also demonstrate the same phenomenon, but mostly with final *-u*, as seen in OB *Gilgameš* (George 2003, 432-433; cf. Pohl 2022, 49-50).

[122] See further Schwemer 2017, 79; George 2003, 433; and especially the study of final vowels in Neo-Babylonian in Hyatt 1941.

[123] On apocopaic final vowels in Late Babylonian, see Jiménez 2017a, 277, with previous literature; cf. Streck 2014, 253-254. For a discussion on final vowels in the Graeco-Babiloniaca, see Streck 2014, 248-252.

[124] On the final vowel *-u* in Late Babylonian literary texts, see Jiménez 2017a, 278, with previous literature.

[125] See also Schwemer 2017, 76.

Logograms

The use of logograms, as is typical of Akkadian literary texts, is limited.[126] Apart from frequently used logograms, such as the names of deities (e.g., ᵈUTU) or common words (e.g., AN ("sky"), KI ("earth"), UN ("people"), etc.), there is one case of a rebus writing in two manuscripts. At 54, *šā'ili* is spelled as *šá*-DINGIR.MEŠ (NinNA2b and BabLBSch8). Additionally, there is an instance of (probably) an erroneous logographic spelling in two manuscripts, both from Sippar. At line 90, the word for "vicious," *zēru*, is rendered with the logogram used for the homonymous *zēru*, "seed," i.e., ŠE.NUMUN.[127]

While there are no distinctive features associated with logographic spelling in the Babylonian manuscripts, in the Assyrian sources, namely the manuscript tradition from Nineveh, the presence or absence of logograms is noteworthy. Above all, NinNA1 appears to employ more logograms compared to other sources from Nineveh, as seen, for example, in ll. 43, 69, 110, and 183. For example, in l. 43, NinNA1 uses the logogram DANNA for *bēru*, contrary to the other NinNA2b. In l. 69, NinNA1 writes [ᵏᵘˢNÍG.N]A₄ for *kīsu*, as attested in NinNA2a. In l. 110, NinNA1 has ᵍⁱˢÉR[IN] instead of *zibānītu*, as in NinNA3b. In l. 183 NinNA1 employs logograms for all the nouns occurring in the line: ᵍⁱˢMUD ᵍⁱˢGAG ᵍⁱˢE₁₁ ᵍⁱˢÁ.⸢SUḪ⸣ (cf. the synoptic transliteration of the text in Rozzi 2021a).

Furthermore, from comparison with the other Assyrian manuscripts, one can suggest that NinNA2(a and b) and NinNA3(a and b) possibly belong to the same tradition. In instances where they both preserve the same lines of text, they often share identical spellings, which deviate from the spellings found in NinNA1. For instance, in line 21, where NinNA2b and NinNA3a preserve the spelling *er-ṣe-ta* for *erṣeta*, NinNA1 has [K]I-*tì*. The different tradition between NinNA1 and NinNA2(a and b) seems to be confirmed by verse 120, where the word *e-lu-ú-ti* in NinNA1 is at odds with the (probably) erroneous variant *el-l*[*u-ú-ti*] in NinNA2a (see further below for text variants). Naturally, these observations remain tentative, since they are based solely on preserved portions of the manuscripts.

In addition, NinNA5 provides an interesting case, as it shows a *nota accusativi*, i.e. a special usage of the preposition *ana* as an accusative marker, often used in Neo-Assyrian (cf. *GAG* §145g; Luukko 2004, 169-170; Jiménez, 2017a, 184; Leonhardt 2024, D.V.2.3). The Assyrian manuscript, although damaged at this point, reads as follows (obv. 5′ // 18 of the hymn): [*mu-šaḫ-miṭ ziq šat ur-r*]*i* ⸢*a-na*⸣ *me-šèr* ⸢ŠE-IM⸣ *na-p*[*iš-ti* x].

Textual Variants

In general, the manuscript tradition does not show significant textual variants, but for some particular cases. Variations among the different manuscripts mostly involve the stem, tense, or mood of verbs, e.g., l. 163 *ikkamsā* in three manuscripts

[126] Streck 2021, 68.
[127] See below for further mistakes in the manuscript tradition of the hymn.

(NinNA1 iii 51; BabLBSch10 obv. 7′; NinNA2a iii 5′), but *kamsā* in SipNBSch1 obv. 1′; l. 165 *pal*[*ḫāka*] in two Assyrian manuscripts (NinNA1 iii 53; NinNA2a iii 7′), but probably *p*[*u-ul*?*-lu*?*-ḫ*]*a*? in the Babylonian SipNBSch1). In some cases, variations are detectable in the suffix pronouns, for example: l. 144 *imaḫḫarka* in two sources, but *imaḫḫarū*, (*i-maḫ-*⌜*ḫa*⌝*-ru*) in AššNASch1 obv. 12′b; *kakkakā-ma* in three manuscripts preserving the l. 91 (NinNA1 ii 24′; NinNA2b ii 10′; SipNB3b ii 8′), but *kakkašū-ma*, written as giš TUKUL-*šu*, in SipNB4a (ii 11′). The presence or absence of the prepositions *ina* or *ana,* or the use of *kī* instead of *kīma* (e.g., l. 121 in NinNA4c ii 5′, whereas NinNA1 iii 9 and SipNB3a iii 16′ have *ki-ma*) also can vary. Given that many of these minor variants are attested in school texts, they likely do not represent different traditions, but rather scribal errors or dialectal features. For example, in the school fragment AššNASch1, obv. 13′b and obv. 14′a (= l. 146), the manuscript preserves *im-ḫa-ru-ka* instead of the expected *im-ḫu-ru-ka*, as found in other manuscripts containing this verse (NinNA1 and SipNB1). As previously observed by Borger, *im-ḫa-ru-ka* could be an Assyrian feature.[128] Another example of variant spelling due to dialectal features is probably ⌜*muš*⌝*-tén-nu-ú* for *muštēnû*, as found in NinNA1 iii 11 (= l. 123).[129]

There are some lexical variants, for example in l. 167, where the term *ṣalipti*, spelled *ṣa-l*[*íp-ti*] in NinNA2a iii 9′, shows the variant *saḫ-maš-t*[*u*₄], "rebellion." (SipNBSch1 obv. 5′). Note, in the same line, the poetic variant of *ṣalipti*, exhibiting an anaptyctic vowel, *ṣal-pa-*⌜*tu*₄⌝ in BabLBSch13, obv. 5′.[130]

There exists, however, one textual variant, that brings about significant changes to the line. Line 159 in the Assyrian sources reads: *ša lamûšināti dannu agû tušēzib attā*, ('You are the one who saved them, surrounded by mighty waves'). Compare the variant reading preserved in a Babylonian school fragment (BabLBSch10): *ša tarammūšināti ina danni ag*[*ê tušēzib attā*] ('You saved from mighty waves those, whom you love"[131]). As noted above, it is difficult to determine whether such a variant is due to an alternative tradition or if it is, instead, merely an error. Considering its attestation in a school manuscript, it is possible that the scribe modified the verse, perhaps because they were writing from memory and therefore remembered it only partially or incorrectly.[132]

[128] Borger 1964, 56. On regressive dissimilation /*u*/ > /*a*/ in Neo-Assyrian, see Luukko 2004, 93 and Leonhardt 2024, B.II.5.1. Note that this school manuscript (VAT 10174) exhibits further Assyrianisms in other excerpts; see Fadhil and Jiménez 2024, *Group 3: School Tablets*.

[129] This represents a case of alternation between a geminated consonant and a long vowel, a common phonological phenomenon in Neo-Assyrian spelling (Luukko 2004, 11 and Leonhardt 2024, A.II.8).

[130] On feminine nouns with anaptyctic vowels see Jiménez 2017a, 77-78.

[131] The translation is my own; cf. Rozzi 2021a. See Jursa, 1999, 101, for the variant line.

[132] On memorization in Sumerian literary texts, with a focus on memorization mistakes in manuscripts of several Sumerian compositions, see Delnero 2012. As remarked by Delnero (2012, p. 191), the process of writing cuneiform tablets could involve direct copying from another tablet, copying from dictation, or copying from memory. According to Delnero's classification, the variant in BabLBSch10 seems to be an error of memorization, of the "substitution"-type. Delnero explains that in most cases erroneous substitutions are substitutions of "[…] a correct word with a synonym […] or with a similar sounding word […]" (Delnero 2012, 196).

Scribal Errors

As previously mentioned, the Hymn to Šamaš was used extensively in the scribal curriculum and has been preserved in numerous school tablets. Therefore, it comes as no surprise that the manuscripts preserving the text occasionally exhibit mistakes and/or textual variants.

The school fragments contain various types of errors, including: phonetic similarity; writing of signs; and omissions. For instance, a phonetic error, possibly due to mishearing during dictation, can be found in a Babylonian manuscript from Sippar (SipNBSch3, obv. 4′), where the unknown term *rug-mu* has replaced the expected and similar-sounding *ruggugu*, "wicked" (l. 127).

Within the same manuscript, the scribe appears to have jumped from line 128 to line 151, an omission that is explainable when one notes that lines 129 and 151 open with the same phrase (*tuštešŝer têrētīšina*). It is likely that the scribe mistakenly switched the two verses because of their similarity. Such an omission is an example of *saut du même au même*. Another possible case of *saut du même au même* is found in verse 149, where the form *adnāti*, though damaged in all the manuscripts that preserve it (NinNA1 iii 37 *ad-na-t*]*i*; NinNA2b iii 9′ ⌜*ad*⌝-[*na-a-ti*; AššNASch1 obv. 15′a [*ad-na*]-*a-ti*, *si vera lectio*), shows the variant *yâti* (spelled *ia-a-tú* in SipNB1 iii 20′), possibly because the word *yâti* appears in the first half of the line immediately preceding (l. 148 ***ana yâti*** *Šamaš uznīšina tušpatti*).[133]

In addition, the Babylonian school fragment BabLBSch4, which comprises the first lines of the hymn (ll. 1-7), shows a possible error in sign similarity. The manuscript displays the corrupt form *ka-la-mu* in the first line (*muš-na-mir gi-mil-lu ka-la-mu*), probably to be understood as *ša*!(KA)-*ma*!(LA)-*mu*, as confirmed by the catchline preserved in some manuscripts of Marduk 1: *mušnammir gimir* ***šá-ma-mu*** (see *supra*).[134]

Nevertheless, some library manuscripts are also not free from mistakes. For example, NinNA2b shows the variant *ana šiddi* instead of *ana ṣibti* (as preserved in other manuscripts) in the first half of line 103. This error is also *a saut du même au même*, since it likely resulted from the similarity between the beginning of line 103 and 105, which both open with the same phrase: *nādin kaspi ana ṣibti* (103); *nādin kaspi ana šiddī* (105). Moreover, NinNA5 exhibits an error of syllable inversion, as it shows the form *me-šèr* instead of *me-reš,* a mistake comparable to the case of *miširtu*/*mešertu* ("produce"), which occasionally shows the variant *mēreštu*, "crop" in divinatory texts, see *CAD* M/2 124.

In summary, the Assyrian textual sources that preserve the Šamaš Hymn exhibit little variation. When comparing manuscripts from Nineveh, NinNA1 appears to differ slightly from NinNA2 and NinNA3, both of which, in turn, seem to belong to the same, or at least a very similar, tradition. NinNA1 appears to

---

[133] Note that instances of *saut du même au même* might occur not only during the act of copying a text, but also, as Worthington (2012, 103) rightly points out, during the process of dictation (including interior dictation). In this case, considering the distance between the lines involved, it could also be explained as a memory error. For further scribal mistakes in this fragment, see Rozzi 2022b.

[134] Cf. Worthington 2012, 92.

employ more logograms than the other Nineveh manuscripts, but overall, the differences are minimal and difficult to confirm due to state of preservation or lack of comparable manuscripts. With a few exceptions (such as the use of *im-ḫa-ru-ka* instead of *im-ḫu-ru-ka* in a manuscript from Assur; see *supra*), there is no evidence of significant dialectal traits or peculiarities.

In the Babylonian manuscript tradition, as expected, school fragments typically exhibit more mistakes and variants. Here, the spellings deviate more from Standard Babylonian, when compared to the Assyrian manuscripts, due to some of the typical features of Babylonian script, such as the preference for vocalization in *-u*.

Style

The Hymno-Epic Dialect

Akkadian hymns are often characterized by the use of a literary style known as the Hymno-Epic Dialect, occasionally found in other literary genres such as epic compositions and disputation poems.[135] Nevertheless, as recently discussed by A. Pohl in her study of Old Babylonian hymns, the Hymno-Epic Dialect is attested in hymnic compositions far more frequently and to a far greater extent than in other texts, so that it might be better considered a "hymnic" idiom.[136] This literary register makes use of archaisms, a vocabulary consisting of rare words often only otherwise attested in lexical lists, rare verbal conjugations (e.g., the ŠD-stem), apocopated personal suffixes, special construct states (in *-u* or *-i*), locative and adverbial endings, and special noun-forms (i.e., nouns with anaptyctic vowels).

The Šamaš Hymn evidences very few Hymno-Epic traits.[137] These amount to: a participle in the ŠD-stem (*mušnammir* ll. 3, 17, 176, 177); few rare words (e.g., *mušemmû*, l. 54, elsewhere unattested[138]); two locatives (*qātukka*, l. 128 and [*ṣ*]*ītukka*, l. 47); examples of the terminative-adverbial ending *-iš* (*eliš u šapliš*, ll. 2, 4, 26; *mitḫāriš*, l. 25);[139] and in one manuscript (NinNA1), a "pseudo" locative ([*š*]*i-ma-tuš*, l. 89[140]).

---

135 For an overview of this literary style, see Jiménez 2017a, 76-79, with fn. 204 for previous literature, especially Lambert 2013, 34-44. Cf. also Hess 2010; cf. recently Pohl 2022, 13ff., on the Hymno-Epic Dialect in Old Babylonian hymns.

136 Pohl 2022, 13, employs the term "register". In fact, the terms "register", or perhaps "idiom", are more suitable than the original term chosen by von Soden (1931 and 1933), i.e. "dialect", since the Hymno-Epic Dialect does not display characteristics determined by regional factors (such as the Assyrian and Babylonian dialects). On this see Lambert 2013, 35.

137 Cf. Lambert 1960b, 48.

138 Cf. Mayer 2017, 11.

139 On the terminative suffix *-iš*, and in particular on *mitḫāriš*, see Mayer 1995.

140 See Mayer 1996, 431.

In contrast, the other Great Hymns and Prayers are characterized by a wider array of Hymno-Epic features, often displaying an almost "baroque" language. Consider, for example, *rigmuški*, "at your cry" (with a peculiar form of the adverbial-locative in *-uš*)[141] in l. 209 of the Literary Prayer to Ištar, or *pisnuqiš*, "wretchedly", in l. 178 of the Nabû Prayer.[142]

Meter

The current scholarly consensus rejects the idea of an Akkadian metrical system based on quantitative or stress patterns, as is found in Latin, Greek, or Arabic verse. Furthermore, there has been significant skepticism toward efforts to segment Akkadian poetry into units based on accentual stress.[143]

Some scholars have attempted to trace similarities between Akkadian poetry and other metric systems.[144] It has also been suggested that Akkadian poetry follows the natural cadence of spoken language and performance. For example, Helle has highlighted the relationship between Akkadian meter and the poetic context (e.g., plot, genre, and figures).[145]

Despite these differences, most scholars now agree that the standard Akkadian meter consists of verses divided into two hemistichs, each forming two metric units. A poetic verse is, therefore, generally composed of a total of four metrical feet. In addition, a metrical caesura falls between the two hemistichs, and is occasionally marked on the tablets by a space or a vertical line. Scholars have termed this verse structure the "*Vierheber*-structure". This metrical model is supported by the materiality of the clay tablets: some Babylonian *Theodicy* manuscripts display vertical lines, which divide each verse into 4 feet.[146] The final foot typically contains a sequence of long and short syllable (i.e., a trochee foot), referred to as the *clausula accadica*.[147] The *clausula accadica* can also be explained as a sequence of a stressed syllable (which usually corresponds to a long syllable) followed by an unstressed one.[148] An example of this *clausula* can also be found in the Šamaš Hymn, especially in those lines where the poetic term for heavens, *šamāmī*, is placed at the end of the line instead of the more common *šamê* (ll. 1, 3,

[141] Cf. Mayer 1996, 434.

[142] For a more detailed analysis of the Hymno-Epic forms occurring in the Great Hymns and Prayers, see Rozzi 2024a. On the use of Hymno-Epic forms in these texts, see also Lambert 1960b, 123; 1982, 176 and 2013, 40.

[143] Wisnom 2015, 485. Cf. West 1997.

[144] Wisnom 2015.

[145] Helle (2014) contends that variations in the metrical scheme depend on the expressiveness of the poetic text. Helle perceives meter as an "independent field of expression", but always in relation to other factors, using it as a vehicle for expressiveness.

[146] Lambert 2013, 22.

[147] For a summary on Akkadian metre (with previous literature), see Jiménez 2017a, 72-75.

[148] Lambert 2013, 18-20.

27, 29). This is probably a deliberate poetic choice, since the word *šamāmī* has a penultimate, stressed syllable and a last, unstressed one.[149]

Verses can also be grouped into stanzas of two (couplets), three (tercets) verses. Stanzas of four verses are also attested and can be analyzed as units of two couplets.[150]

The strophic division, often marked by horizontal rulings, is particularly common in hymns,[151] and the most common verse-grouping is the couplet.[152]

Akkadian meter is principally influenced by the syntax of the language rather than by metrical ictus. Each foot is typically formed by a word or by a phrase (e.g., a genitive chain), although there are exceptions.[153] Individual poetic lines are generally composed of self-contained and grammatically independent phrases.[154] In Akkadian poetry, meter is closely connected to other poetic devices. Indeed, verses, in any type of stanza, are often arranged according to parallelism. That is, parallelisms across two verses, or across two couplets, and even within the same verse (i.e., across two hemistichs), are commonly attested (see *infra*: *Parallelism*).[155]

As mentioned above, Šamaš Hymn has a distinct layout, typical of the other Great Hymns, with a division into poetic couplets.[156] This structural feature is evident in all the Nineveh manuscripts, as well as in certain Babylonian manuscripts (e.g., SipNB3a), where a horizontal line is drawn every two verses to delineate couplets. As noted previously above, the division into couplets is not always regular, and sometimes the manuscripts show stanzas of three verses (tercets) instead of two (e.g., ll. 107-109).

A metrical analysis of the Šamaš Hymn reveals that the basic metrical pattern shows numerous variations within the composition. Despite most lines being standard "*Vierheber*" verses, there are also lines that consist of only three metrical units, or in longer verses, up to seven units.[157]

---

[149] Cf. Lambert 2013, 20; Jiménez 2017a, 227; Fadhil and Jiménez 2022, 257.

[150] Four-verses stanzas are attested for example in Old Babylonian hymns, see e.g. the Ammiditana's hymn to Ištar (Thureau-Dangin 1925).

[151] Hess 2015, 262.

[152] Jiménez 2017a, 73, with further references.

[153] E.g., some words linked together in merismatic pairs can also form a single foot (see Jiménez 2017a, 73 fn. 190, and Lambert 2013 for more information on metric feet).

[154] Hess 2015, 262.

[155] See Jiménez 2017a, 73-74.

[156] Many manuscripts of the compositions referred to as Marduk 1 and Marduk 2, as well as the manuscripts of the Great Nabû Hymn, exhibit the same characteristic layout.

[157] I base my analysis on Lambert 2013, 17-28. For the precise metrical pattern in each line, see the online edition in Rozzi 2021a, where the metric feet and caesura are marked in the transcription. I use here the same conventions as in the eBL edition, that is: every foot is divided with a vertical line ('|'); the metrical break is rendered with two vertical lines ('||'); and uncertain division (metric division between two nouns is uncertain), is rendered with '(|)'. In the present text, 131 lines display the standard '*Vierheber*-structure', with a metrical break in the middle. That is, they are regular 2+2 lines. Some lines might be interpreted as 2+2, or 2+1, where "bound pairs of words" (Lambert 2013, 23), which can be understood as one or two units, occur. Consider, e.g., l. 26: *attā-ma* | *nāqissina* || (*ša*) *eliš* (|) *u šapliš*. Further cases of uncertain 2+2 verses are, e.g., l. 34 (which could be also interpreted as 3+2), l. 36 (2+1), and l. 171 (perhaps

In this respect, and although irregular verses display a relatively even distribution throughout the text, the central section – characterized by a "wisdom" or "gnomic" rather than a "hymnic" tone – is striking for having the highest concentration of non-standard verses. For instance, verses 99, 107, and 112 appear to consist of only two metrical units (1+1), while verses 92, 114, 116, and 122 seem to have three. Additionally, verses 105 and 118 appear hypermetrical, with perhaps 6 and 7 feet respectively.

Furthermore, l. 93 employs a technique to avoid too short a verse-end: the introduction of an additional, superfluous element into the line – e.g., an independent pronoun – to create a metrical unit: *ina pî* (|) *dayāni* | *ul ippalū* || ***šunu*** | *aḫḫūšu*. In this case, the independent pronoun *šunu* is seemingly unnecessary, from either a syntactical or semantic perspective. It serves neither to provide greater emphasis, nor is explainable grammatically. Instead, it appears solely to maintain a balanced four-beat verse structure. Nevertheless, the verse immediately preceding it appears "truncated," with only three feet.[158]

The hymn's *incipit*, the conclusion, and, in general, verses that align with the traditional hymnic style (i.e., the use of epithets or participles; see *supra* for the structure of the hymn) exhibit a more structured meter.

The variation in scansion between the central wisdom section and the more "hymnic" portions of the text is accompanied by a diversity of themes, style, and vocabulary. This may provide further evidence to support the hypothesis that the text was composed in several different stages, potentially incorporating disparate texts.

As mentioned above, in addition to the typical hymnic division into poetic couplets, the composition also displays a so-called *a-a'* structure: two sets of identical verses are repeated, with the god's name introduced in the second stanza. This stylistic device can sometimes affect the meter, since the addition of the divine name adds an extra metrical foot. In this regard, one notes that the first verse consists of only three units: *mušnammir* || *gimir* (|) *šamāmī* (i.e., a 1+2 structure, or even 1+1). The irregularity in the metre is then resolved in the third verse, where the name of Šamaš, in the first half of the line, balances the metric division and creates the standard *Vierheber* (2+2): ***Šamaš*** | *mušnammir* || *gimir* (|) *šamāmī*.

Figurative Language

It is difficult to fully ascertain the nuances of certain poetic features in Akkadian and Sumerian literary texts, particularly those related to rhythm, recitation, and

1+1). Indeed, as shown by Lambert (2013, 24) in his metrical analysis of *Enūma eliš*, other schemes that do not align with the standard 2+2 pattern are also possible, such as 3+2, 2+1 or 1+2. In the Šamaš Hymn, an example of a line with a 1+2 pattern can be found in l. 8: *iriššūka* || *gimiršunu* | *igīgū*. Line 43 shows a 3+2 pattern: *ana šiddī* | *ša lā idî* | *nesûti* || *u* (*ana*) *bērī* | *lā man*[*ûti*]. Some longer lines show an unusual meter, raising doubts that they should be analyzed as poetry, and instead be considered prose (e.g., l. 62 (4+2?); l. 118 (3+4?)).

[158] For the example here and additional instances of this poetic phenomenon in other texts, see Lambert 2013, 27.

musical performance.[159] Nevertheless, it is evident that the Hymn to Šamaš employs numerous poetic devices.

The most noticeable trait of this hymn, upon first reading, is the tendency towards repetition.

Described by Vogelzang as a "goldmine" for repetition,[160] the Hymn to Šamaš is characterized by various types of repetition, including rhyme, assonance, consonance, and the *a-a'* structure. A further device occurring in the text, which uses repetition and affects the syntax of the verses, is anaphora. Other syntactic devices in this hymn include anastrophe, enjambement, and parallelism. The latter is the most frequently used rhetorical device in the Šamaš Hymn. The text is also rich in metaphors and similes.

Phonological Figures

Although the original recitation of the hymn is lost to us, some verses clearly exhibit deliberate sound repetitions. Indeed, the Hymn to Šamaš features various phonological figures, including assonance, consonance, alliteration, and rhyme.[161]

Identifying rhyme in Akkadian literary texts is particularly challenging. Rhyme, which is the repetition of the same phonemes at the end of a verse, within the same verse (here: homoeoteleuton)[162] or even between words across multiple verses, is not a commonly used or appreciated poetic device in Akkadian poetry. Some scholars even suggest that rhyme is often deliberately avoided.[163] Consequently, determining whether a rhyme is intentional or coincidental is

---

[159] Cf. Michalowski 1996, 144. For a general definition of figurative language, and a brief description of the tropes and schemes that will be mentioned in the following paragraphs, see Abrams and Harpham 2014; Lanham 1991; Sloane 2001; and Lausberg 1998. See Watson 1986; 1999, for a classification of rhetorical devices in Hebrew, Ugaritic, and Akkadian poetry. See also the recent treatment of Akkadian "persuasion" strategies, with a list of previous works engaging with Akkadian rhetorical and poetic devices, by Piccin 2021. For a more detailed overview of rhetoric in Mesopotamian literature, with further examples of rhetorical devices in Akkadian literary texts, and specifically in the *Great Hymns and Prayers*, see Rozzi 2024a, Chapter 5.

[160] Vogelzang 1996, 177: "The whole of the *Shamash Hymn* turns out to be a goldmine when one is searching for forms of general patterning by repetition".

[161] For the definition and explanation of phonological figures, see Plett 2010, 97ff.

[162] The rhyme occurring within the same verse of a poem can also be defined "internal rhyme", see Cuddon 1998, 423-424. However, I use here the term "rhyme" to denote the most common type of rhyme, i.e., the end rhyme (Cuddon 1998, 260). Rhyme is a type of homoeoteleuton. The term "homoeoteleuton" (Cuddon 1998, 386) more generally denotes any rhyme between words that end in the same way, either at the end of the verse or between contiguous words, and between stressed or unstressed syllables. I will here describe as cases of homoeoteleuton words that share the same or a similar ending, stressed or unstressed, and do not constitute end rhymes. For the sake of concision, I will not distinguish here between homoeoteleuton and homoioptoton. For the difference between homoeoteleuton and homoioptoton, see Lanham 1991, 83-85. For further attestations of both homoeoteleuton and homoioptoton in Akkadian literature, see Pohl 2022, 77-78. Cf. also Rozzi 2024a.

[163] Wasserman 2002, 157.

difficult. For instance, in ll. 190-193, the repetition of the possessive suffix *-ka* at the end of lines creates a rhyming sound. However, this is likely unintentional and the result of the Akkadian language itself (*-ka* being the most common means of expressing a 2nd person masculine singular possessive suffix).

Despite these challenges, there are a few cases where it seems reasonable to assume that the poet intentionally created a rhyming structure or some sort of sound effect. The following are some examples of phonological rhetorical figures found in the text:

- Assonance (i.e., the repetition of vowel sounds in closely placed words) in l. 113 *nādin šīqāti ana birīyi* (*lā*) *mušaddin atri*[164] (note the repetition of the vowels /*a*/ and /*i*/); a similar assonance can be observed in l. 110, despite the end of the line being broken: *ša kīni ṣābit zibānīti mādā* [...] (/*a*/ and /*i*/);
- Consonance (the repetition of consonant sounds within or at the end of closely placed words) in l. 78: *taparras ar*[*kāt*]*i taše*ʾʾ*e napšāti*?. Here the repetition of the phonemes /*t*/ and /*r*/ in the first hemistich, and /*t*/ and /*š*/ in the second, can be adduced. Furthermore, the same line demonstrates the use of assonance through the repetition of the vowel /*a*/,: ...*arkāti* / ...*napšāti*. There are numerous examples of lines that display a combination of different phonological devices, e.g., l. 43, which exhibits assonance, consonance and homoeoteleuton: *ana šiddī ša lā idî nesûti u ana bērī lā man*[*ûti*]. The first hemistich shows the repetition of /*š*/ and /*d*/ and the vowels /*a*/ and /*i*/. The end of the first and second hemistich (... *nesûti* /... *man*[*ûti*]) forms a homoeoteleuton. L. 186 offers a further example of both assonance and consonance: [... *ṭ*]*ēmi mitluki šitūlti milki*. The reiteration of the vowels /*u*/ and /*i*/ and of the consonances /*m*/, /*l*/, /*t*/ and /*k*/ is clearly deliberate.
- Homoeoteleuton: l. 156 *ina ešrê* ***rīšāta illata*** *u ḫidâti*, note furthermore the consonance and assonance resulting from the repetition of /a/ and /t/; l. 177 *pētû ek****leti*** *mušnammir er****ṣeti*** *rapašti*, also here the homoeoteleuton is enriched by the consonance, due to the repetition of /t/. In addition, a more complex kind of homoeoteleuton occurs in ll. 148-149, where the same phoneme is repeated both within the same line (l. 148) and across the couplet (ll. 148-149): (148) *ana* ***yâti*** *šamaš lā tazêršin****āti*** / (149) *ša ad*[***nā***]***ti*** *šamaš uznīšina tušpatti.*
- Rhyme: rhyming couplets are found, for examples, in ll. 190-193, which all end with the suffix *-ka*; however, as mentioned above, it is difficult to say whether these types of rhymes are intentional or not. Nevertheless, an identical rhyme can be found between ll. 177 and 179, which both end with *erṣeti rapašti*.
- Alliteration, where the same consonant is repeated at the beginning of closely placed words, can be found in l. 39: *šad*[*ī*?] *kīma qê kasâta kīma imbari katmāta* (repetition of the phoneme /k/ and homoeoteleuton between *kasâta* and *katmāta*); note also l. 71: *munnabta munnarba māḫāzī tukallam* (repetition of /*m*/). Note, furthermore, the assonance in this line, rendered through the repetition of /*u*/ and /*a*/. See also l. 128 [*m*]*anāma* (*u*) *mamma puqqudu qātukka*. Here there is alliteration of /*m*/ in the first half of the line, and consonance of /*q*/ and /*k*/ in the second. Assonance is also achieved through the repetition of the vowels /*a*/ and /*u*/.

[164] The particle *lā* is written here in brackets since it appears as a variant in one manuscript from Sippar (SipNB4a). It is probably a mistake.

Syntactic Figures

The Hymn to Šamaš shows several figures of syntax, that is, figures of speech that modify the structure of sentences.[165]

Anaphora, i.e., the repetition of a word or phrase at the beginning of successive clauses or verses, occurs very often. Consider ll. 124-125:

> ***šūt*** *lumni īpušū zēršunu u[l dāri*?*]*
> ***šūt*** *ulla pīšunu šakin ina maḫrīka*
>
> The seed of evildoers shall n[ot abide].
> The nay-sayers' testimonies are before you.

Other cases of anaphora are attested in ll. 92-94 (repetition of the preposition *ina*), ll. 114-115 (repetition of *ina lā...*), ll. 154-155 (repetition of *mala*), ll.169-170 (repetition of *šūt*), and ll. 174-175 (repetition of *ayūtu/ayātu*).

The text makes significant use of anastrophe. Anastrophe is a rhetorical device that involves inverting or rearranging the typical word order of a sentence. In Akkadian literary texts of different genres, both prose and poetry, the standard order of words can be altered (in poetry occasionally for metric purposes). For instance, the verb, which typically occupies the end of the sentence, can be placed in the penultimate position to ensure a trochaic ending. Nouns and adjectives can also be inverted. Anastrophe is also associated with the phenomenon of "fronting," where the verb is positioned at the beginning of the sentence.[166] Examples of anastrophe in the Šamaš Hymn are:

- Verb in penultimate position: l. 36 [*ša*?] *igīgī lā īdû qereb libbīša*;
- Fronting: l. 16 *uštep[per]ā ana nūrī[ka] gimiršina mātātu*;
- Verb in penultimate position and inversion of the noun/adjective: l. 28 [*š*]*umdulta erṣeta tabâʾ ūmīšam*.

A particularly interesting case of anastrophe is found in l. 17: *mušnammir pētû ekleti ṣerret šam[āmī]*, which should be read instead, *mušnammir ekleti pētû ṣerret šamāmī* ("Illuminator of darkness, opener of the bosom of heaven").[167]

---

[165] On the definition of syntactic figures, see Plett 2010, 183ff.

[166] For the placing of verbs in the penultimate position, see Groneberg 1987, 175-179; for the use of this device in Akkadian hymns see Pohl 2022, 55-61; for its use in epic see Hecker 1974, 1201-38; George 2003, 433-434. For the inversion of adjective and noun, see George 2003, 434; Pohl 2022, 55-57. For the placement of the verb at the beginning of the line, see Groneberg 1987, 176-177. See also Schwemer 2014, 279, for examples of 'fronting' in first-millennium Akkadian incantations. Cf. also several occurrences of *hyperbaton* (the separation of a verb and its predicate) in the Babylonian disputation *Palm and Vine* (ed. Jiménez 2017a, 281-282).

[167] See Borger 1964, 55.

Enjambement is rare in Akkadian literature, but can occasionally be found in poetry, when subordination is particularly complex.[168] In the Šamaš Hymn, there are several examples:

> ll. 29-30:
> *mīl tâmti ḫursānī erṣeta šamāmī*
> *kī takkassi ginâ tabâʾ ūmīšam*
>
> High seas, mountains, earth, and sky,
> You traverse them regularly, every day, as if they were pavement.

Further examples of enjambement can be found in ll. 122-123, ll. 130-131, ll. 133-134, and ll. 168-173.

Parallelism

Numerous studies have examined parallelism in Akkadian literature, yet a comprehensive study of this phenomenon remains a *desideratum*.[169] Parallelism is the most prevalent rhetorical device in Semitic literatures and is also extensively used in Akkadian compositions. It is especially common in Wisdom Literature,[170] but is a typical poetic feature of the hymnic genre as well.[171]

To illustrate the use of parallelism in the hymn under consideration, I follow the model proposed by Streck in his study of parallelism in the Old Babylonian hymns,[172] presenting examples of synthetic, antithetic, and synonymous parallelisms.[173]

---

[168] Groneberg 1987, 176 and 184; Westenholz 1997, 192.

[169] For further reading on parallelism in Akkadian sources, see Berlin 1979; cf. Berlin 1992; see also Foster 2005, 14-16 and Streck 2007. For a detailed description of parallelism in Old Babylonian hymns, see Pohl 2022, 79-86. For some reflections on parallelism in the Hymn to Šamaš and in other Akkadian literary texts, see De Zorzi 2022. Furthermore, note that the ERC project (ERC-2018-STG, 2019-2024) "Repetition, parallelism and creativity: an inquiry into the construction of meaning in Ancient Mesopotamian literature and erudition" (REPAC), is currently being conducted at the University of Vienna (PI: De Zorzi). A comprehensive study on parallelism in Akkadian and Ugaritic poetry at the end of the second millennium is in preparation (Steinberger forthcoming).

[170] Donald 1966, 315.

[171] See, e.g., the list of all the occurrences of parallelism in the Old Babylonian Hymns in Streck 2007, 180-181.

[172] Streck 2007, 167-184; see more recently Pohl 2022, 79-86.

[173] This classification is simplified and serves only to briefly illustrate the variety of parallelisms encountered in the Šamaš Hymn. In short, synthetic parallelism provides an expansion, varying the already expressed concept and adding a new element; antithetic parallelism juxtaposes two opposing concepts, creating a contrast; and synonymous parallelism repeats the same concept twice, identically or almost identically. Other types of parallelism include grammatical parallelism (see Annus and Lenzi 2000, who defines it as a parallelism in which "almost every slot in each line is mirrored in the other"), and phonological parallelism, where the parallelism is based on phonetic equivalence. For examples of grammatical parallelism in our hymn, see ll.

Parallelism in the Hymn to Šamaš is built in various ways: within two verses, across more than two verses, or even within a single verse. Although one mostly observes couplets forming synthetic parallelisms[174], the structure of the text itself, especially the central portion focusing on ethical issues, is essentially antithetic, contrasting just and unjust behavior.

A parallelism of the synonymous type is found in the very first lines of the text (ll.1-4), as well as in ll. 5-6:

saḫpū kīma šuškalli erṣeta šarūrūka
ša ḫuršāni bērūti eṭûtīšunu tušpardi

Your radiance spreads out like a net over the world,
You brighten the gloom of the distant mountains.

The rulings on two manuscripts (NinNA1 and NinNA2) match the parallelism, coupling ll. 5-6 together. Another clear instance of synonymous parallelism occurs in ll. 120-121:

urappaš kimta mešrâ irašši
kīma mê nagbi dārî zēr[*šu*] *dā*[*ri*]

He shall make (his) family numerous, he shall build up wealth,
[His] seed shall be perpe[tual] as the waters of a perpetual spring.

Here the parallel couplet appears to be divided by a horizontal ruling in two of the four manuscripts that preserve the line (NinNA1 and SipNB3a). An antithetic parallelism occurs in ll. 59-60:

arikta napišti ragg[*i t*]*usāq u tuš*[*akri*]
ireḫḫīšum-ma šitta kīma ṣālili inappu[*š kīnu*]

You give [short] shrift to the wicked,
Slumber creeps over the [just], he breathes like a man in repose.

169-170, where both verses begin with the pronoun *šūt*, followed by a verb in the 3rd person plural, or the series of lines at the end of the text, all beginning with a participle (ll. 176-184). For further types of parallelism, see Berlin 1992, 154-162. Cf. Streck 2007, 172-173.

174 I identify the following synthetic parallelisms: ll. 7-8, 11-12, 13-14, 17-18, 21-22, 29-30, 31-32, 33-34, 35-36, 37-38, 43-44, 47-48, 49-50, 53-56 (four line parallelism), 65-66, 67-68, 69-70, 71-72, 73-74, 77-78, 79-80, 83-84, 85-87 (three line parallelism), 88-89, 90-91, 92-94 (three line parallelism), 95-96, 97-98, 99-100, 101-102, 103-104, 105-106, 107-109 (three line parallelism), 110-111, 112-115 (four line parallelism), 116-117, 118-119, 124-125, 126-127, 128-129, 132-134 (three line parallelism), 135-137 (three line parallelism), 138-139, 140-141, 142-143, 144-145, 146-147, 149-150, 160-161, 167-173 (multiple line parallelism), 180-181, 186-187, 188-189, 190-191, 192-194 (uncertain due to broken line), 195-196, 197-198, 199-200. Note, however, that the distinction between synonymous and synthetic parallelisms is very loose. Cf. Streck 2007, 173.

A synthetic parallelism can be found in ll. 95-96:

ša kāṣir anzilli qarnāšu tuballa
ēpiš šiddi kāpida eni qaqqaršu

You blunt the horns of the contriver of offenses,
The swindler plotting to work a draw, his foothold's undercut.

A synthetic parallelism that extends across multiple lines and creates a so-called "envelope figure"[175] can be observed between lines 149-153. In these verses, the image of Šamaš illuminating the world and delivering just verdicts in divinatory practices, thus ensuring wisdom for humankind, is articulated. The five lines develop these motifs, repeating them with minor variations.

A further example of a synonymous parallelism stretched over three lines is found between ll. 132-134 (note also the enjambement between ll. 133-134):

ana ḫurri pîšu dunnamû išassīka
ulālu enšu ḫubbulu muškēnu
ummisalla (ina) masdara ginâ imaḫḫarka

The feeble one calls you as much as his speech allows him,
The meek, the weak, the oppressed, the wretched,
Daily, always, and steadily appeal to you.

In l. 180, one finds an example of synthetic parallelism built within a single line: *mukarrû ūmī* || *murrik mušâti*, "Who can shorten the days and lengthen the nights".

As previously stated, the central part of the hymn, the so-called "wisdom" section, consists of opposing parallel verses that together form an antithetical structure. Examples of honest and dishonest conduct are contrasted, creating a complex sequence of antitheses. This pattern is clearly visible in verses 97-109, which comprise a series of couplets – and, finally, a triplet – of synthetic parallelisms. Each couplet contrasts with that which immediately follows it, creating an antithetic structure.

The division into couplets is regularly marked by horizontal rulings on library manuscripts (NinNA1, NinNA2b, SipNB3b, SipNB4a). A break occurs only in the triplet (ll. 107-109), where, after verse 107 (which logically belongs with the other two), a ruling is drawn:

dayāna ṣalpa mēsera tukallam
māḫir ṭāti lā muštēšira tušazbal arna
You show the roguish judge (the inside of) a jail,
He who takes the fee but does not carry through, you make him bear the punishment.

---

175 "Inclusio or envelope figure is the repetition of the same words at the beginning and end of a section of poetry" (Watson 1994, 353). Both l. 149 and l. 153 of the Hymn to Šamaš end with the same phrase: *uznīšina tušpatti*.

lā māḫir ṭāti ṣābit(u) abbūt enši
ṭāb eli šamaš balāṭa uttar
The one who receives no fee but takes up the cause of the weak,
Šamaš is pleased with him, he will prolong (his) life.

dayānu muštālu ša dīn mīšari idīnu
ugammar ēkalla šubat rubê mūšabšu
The scrupulous judge who gives just verdicts,
He will have a palace at his disposal, princely will be his dwelling.

nādin kaspi ana ṣibti ḫābilu mīnâ uttar
uštakaṣṣab ana nēmelim-ma uḫallaq kīsa
What return will there be for the exploitive lender of money?
He will cause a decrease in profit and he will lose the principal.

nādin kaspi ana šiddī rūqūti mutēr ištēn šiqli ana šelal[*ti*]
ṭāb eli Šamaš balāṭa ut[*tar*]
He who invests long-term, who returns one shekel for thr[ee],
Šamaš is pleased with him, he will pro[long] (his) life.

ṣābit zibānīti ēpiš ṣilipti
muštēnû aban kīsi ušaqqa (*u*) *ušappal*
uštakaṣṣab ana nēmelim-ma uḫal[*laq kīsa*]
He who cheats as he holds the scales,
Who switches weights, making them more or less,
He will cause a decrease in profit and he will lose the [principal].

In these stanzas, note, furthermore, the pun occurring at the beginning of ll. 98-99 (***māḫir ṭāti lā*** *muštēšira*... / *lā māḫir ṭāti* ...) and the *figura etymologica* in line 101.[176]

Metaphors and Similes

A simile is a figure of speech that explicitly compares two distinctly different things using specific particles (e.g., "like" or "as"). In the Akkadian language, such comparisons are made using particles such as *kī*, *kīma*, or the terminative-adverbial suffix *-iš*. In contrast, a metaphor uses a word or expression that denotes one thing to refer to something entirely different, without making an explicit comparison. The shared quality or characteristic between the two elements in a simile or metaphor is called *tertium comparationis*.[177] In the Hymn to Šamaš, almost all similes are

[176] A *figura etymologica* is a rhetorical device, in which words that are etymologically related are used together in a phrase or sentence. These words may belong to different parts of speech, such as a verb and a noun. See Plett 2010, 174.

[177] For metaphors in Akkadian literature see Streck 1999; for similes see Wasserman 2002, 99-156; see also the recent treatment of similes in the Assyrian Royal Inscription provided by Bach

expressed using *kīma*,[178] in contrast to other Great Hymns and Prayers, where the terminative suffix *-iš* is often used as an alternative.[179] In the text under study, metaphors and similes can involve elements of the natural world, humans and abstract nouns.[180]

Metaphors

- Nature: l. 17 *ṣerret šam*[*āmī*], "the bosom of heavens", for the clouds (cf. the commentary to this line); l. 18 *napiš*[*ti*] *māti*, "the life of the land", for the grain fields;
- *Abstracta*: l. 40 *rapšu andullaka*, "Your broad protection", for the sunrays; l. 87 *tarṣat šētka rappu ina erṣeti kamār*[*um-ma*?] "Your net is spread, a snare in the earth, a *hunting trap* [*indeed*!]", all three nouns as metaphors for the sunrays.

Similes

- Nature: l. 39 *kīma imbari katmāta,* "you [bl]anket them (i.e., the mountains) like a haze"; l. 179 *mušaḫmiṭ kīma nabli*, "Who makes (the wide world) glow like flame"; l. 121 *kīma mê nagbi dārî zēr*[*šu*] *dā*[*ri*], "[His] seed shall be perpe[tual] as the waters of a perpetual spring" (note the polyptoton[181] in: ... *dārî* / *dā*[*ri*]);
- *Abstracta*: l 30 *kī takkassi ginâ tabâʾ ūmīšam,* "You traverse them regularly, every day, as if they were pavement."

In this hymn, it is possible to observe a construction that, while employing a comparative marker, does not strictly function as a simile. Instead, it represents what is known as a "literal comparison." A literal comparison does not imply any figurative or metaphorical meaning but rather presents a purely factual comparison between two elements based on their actual qualities.[182] An example of this can be found in line 60: *ireḫḫīšum-ma šitta kīma ṣālili inappu*[*š kīnu*], "Slumber creeps over the [just], he breathes like a man in repose."[183]

2021; cf. also Pohl 2022, 68-71 for a comprehensive catalogue of similes and metaphors in the Old Babylonian hymns.

[178] Only in l. 30, in the only manuscript that preserves the beginning of the line (NinNA2b i 14′), is the simile expressed by the particle *kī*: *ki-i* ⸢*ták-kàs*⸣*-si*. It is therefore impossible to say whether the other manuscripts also used *kī* or *kīma* instead.

[179] E.g., in the Ištar Prayer, l. 193 (broken context): *iṣṣūriš*, "like a bird"; or the prayer to Ištar Anūna: l. 106 *ḫabīliš*, "like a criminal"; see Rozzi 2024a for further examples.

[180] It should be noted that the following list is not exhaustive and only serves to illustrate some examples.

[181] Polyptoton is a rhetorical device where the same root word is repeated in different forms or grammatical cases within the same sentence or passage.

[182] On this construction in Akkadian literary texts, see Wasserman 2003, 100 with further references.

[183] I am grateful to J. Bach for pointing out this example.

Vocabulary

The lexicon of the *Great Hymn to Šamaš* is undoubtedly poetic and sophisticated, yet distinct from the often obscure vocabulary of other Great Hymns and Prayers. Overall, the text lacks the highly epigrammatic style of Marduk 1 and Marduk 2, and the *hapaxes* and unusual words found in the *Great Prayer to Nabû* and the *Great Prayer to Ištar*.[184] Unlike the *Gula Hymn of Bullussa-rabi* and the *Syncretistic Hymn to Gula*, it does not use erudite references and epithets based on religious and mythological themes. Only one verse of the Hymn to Šamaš is quoted in commentaries. Against this, compare, for example, Marduk 2, which has its own commentary, in which the difficult terms used in the text are explained.[185]

The Hymn to Šamaš is not devoid of learned words or rare formulations (such as the uncertain *ēpiš šiddi* in l. 96, for example), but it does not exhibit the same degree of lexical complexity as other compositions. This aspect, along with the general scarcity of Hymno-Epic traits, distinguishes the style of the Hymn to Šamaš from the other Great Hymns and Prayers.

In addition, Lambert noted the use of some typically Old Babylonian terms and phrases (e.g. *šīqu* in l. 113; cf. *CAD* Š/3, 102),[186] which further suggests that the composition of the hymn might have occurred in several phases, with the original kernel possibly dating back to the Old Babylonian period.

Conclusion

The Šamaš Hymn is a sophisticated literary work, notable for its rich rhetorical elements, its elevated language, and its extensive central section devoted to the themes of Wisdom Literature. Although determining the exact date of its composition is challenging, it is likely that the text was originally composed during the Old Babylonian period, with gradual modification and expansion over time. The original *Sitz im Leben* of the hymn remains unclear, but its widespread use and inclusion in educational curricula suggest that it was highly valued and considered an important text for the training of the scribal elite.[187] The hymn's content, which

[184] See in the Nabû prayer the rare words *mukkallu* (l. 40), a kind of priest, l. 71 *taltaltu*, perhaps an otherwise unattested female variant of *taltallu*, "pollen"; in the Ištar Prayer, see, e.g., l. 84 *anūnu*, a literary term for "fear".

[185] Jiménez 2017b.

[186] Lambert 1960a, 321.

[187] Wisdom literature in Mesopotamia fulfilled an educational function by imparting fundamental life skills, moral teachings, and theological insights. In doing so, it played a crucial role in preserving and transmitting the traditional ideology and cultural values of Mesopotamian civilization, equipping individuals, particularly the learned elite, with the knowledge to navigate the complexities of existence and fulfill their societal roles. On the intellectual context of Wisdom Literature and its importance in education, see Beaulieu 2007; Cohen 2013, 17; Cohen and Wasserman 2021, 124. See in particular the remarks by Cohen 2013, 76, with respect to the

blends religious and wisdom themes, may have contributed to its appeal among intellectual circles. Interestingly, the hymn lacks any clear references to a cultic or liturgical setting. This could imply that it was primarily intended as a literary work. Perhaps it also served as a model of refined composition, studied and preserved within the scribal tradition for its artistic and intellectual merit, rather than for ritual or cultic use.[188]

---

importance of Wisdom Literature in the scribal education: "Perhaps rather than maintaining an image of wisdom solely learned for the sake of morally improving oneself, we should also think of wisdom as a means of achieving scribal education and erudition, and on a higher level, as a source of exegesis, just as the book of Proverbs was used in Talmud tractates to explicate select passages from the Bible."

[188] The significance of this hymn as a wisdom text is further reinforced by its intertextual connections with other works of Wisdom Literature, as previously discussed in this study. Notably, its quotation in the "parodic" *Dialogue of Pessimism* – although the parodic nature of this composition is debated (see Foster 1974, 81-82) – demonstrates the hymn's importance and popularity within the scribal community. This also highlights its role in the broader intellectual and literary tradition of the time. A parodic quotation, in particular, suggests that the quoted text was well-known enough to be recognized and even subverted, similar to the parodic use of the *Theodicy* observed in the Babylonian Disputation Poems (see Jiménez 2018, especially p. 130: "The position of the Theodicy as a superlatively learned poem, written by a celebrated ancient scholar during a golden age of Mesopotamian *belles lettres* and reserved only for scribes who had reached the peak of their art, meant that it was almost inevitable that it came to be parodied by the very tradition that hallowed it." Cf. also Jiménez 2017a, 105, on the same topic: "The humor lies in the contrast between the original solemn context of the formula and its new, preposterous use: the recognition of the hypotext is thus key for the parodic effect").

Manuscripts

NINEVEH	
NinNA1	K 3182+ (Brünnow 1889, 28-32; Gray 1901a, 132-133; 1901b pl. 1, 2; *BWL*, pls. 33, 34; Rozzi 2022b, 153-154)
NinNA2a	K 3650 (Brünnow 1889, 33-34; *BWL*, pl. 35, 36)
NinNA2b	K 3474 + K 8233 + Sm 372 (Brünnow 1889, 25-27 and 35; *BWL*, pl. 35, 36)
NinNA3a	Sm 1033 (Gray 1901a, 242; 1901b pl. 19; *BWL*, pl. 33, 34, 35)
NinNA3b	1883,0118.472 (*BWL*, pl. 33, 34, 35)
NinNA3c	K 19543 (Rozzi, 2021b, 218)
NinNA4a	BM 98631 (*BWL*, pl. 34)
NinNA4b	BM 98732 (*BWL*, pl. 33)
NinNA4c	BM 134517 (*CTL* 1, no. 131)
NinNA5	K 10866 (*BWL*, pl. 33)
NinNA6	K 20637 (*CTL* 1, no. 132)
ASSUR	
AššNA1	IM 148526 (Fadhil forthcoming)
AššNASch1	VAT 10174 (*KAR* 321; *KAL* 15, no. 33; *BWL*, pl. 36)
AššNASch2	VAT 10071 (*KAL* 15, no. 29; *BWL*, pl. 73)
AššNASch3	VAT 10756 (*KAL* 15, no. 30; *BWL*, pl. 73)
BABYLON	
BabNB1	BM 38849 (Rozzi 2022b, 153; Leichty, Finkel and Walker 2019, 404)
BabNB2	BM 39096 (Rozzi 2023, 156; Leichty, Finkel and Walker 2019, 410)
BabNB3	1880,0617.2987[189]
BabLBSch1	BM 33465+ (*CTL* 1, no. 137; Rozzi 2021, 220; Leichty, Finkel and Walker 2019, 209[190])
BabLBSch2	BM 33769 (Geller 1997, 94)
BabLBSch3	BM 35077 (*CTL* 1, no. 138; Leichty, Finkel and Walker 2019, 277)
BabLBSch4	BM 36296 + BM 38070 (*CTL* 1, no. 135; Leichty, Finkel and Walker 2019, 317 and 379)
BabLBSch5	BM 37122 (*CTL* 1, no. 136; Leichty, Finkel and Walker 2019, 349)
BabLBSch6	BM 37502 (*CTL* 1, no. 139; Leichty, Finkel and Walker 2019, 362)
BabLBSch7	BM 38061 (Rozzi 2021b, 218; Gesche 2001, 685; Leichty, Finkel and Walker 2019, 379)
BabLBSch8	BM 38167 (Rozzi 2021b, 214-215 no. 1; Leichty, Finkel and Walker 2019, 383)
BabLBSch9	BM 40080 (*CTL* 1, no. 134; Leichty, Finkel and Walker 2019, 433)
BabLBSch10	BM 42652 (*CTL* 1, no. 133; Leichty, Finkel and Walker 2019, 523)
BabLBSch11	BM 54569 (Lambert 2013, 541)

[189] Identification by Zs. Földi. It will be edited by the author in a future publication.
[190] A new fragment belonging to this manuscript has been recently identified by Zs. Földi: BM 48914. It will be edited by the author in a future publication.

BabaLBSch12	BM 101558 (*CTL* 1, no. 140; Gesche 2001, 665; George and Bongenaar 2002, 155)
BabLBSch13	VAT 17553 (*CTL* 1, no. 142)
BabLBSch14	BM 37287 (Rozzi 2022b, 154-155; Leichty, Finkel and Walker 2019, 355)
BabLBSch15	BM 48214 + BM 48226 (Rozzi 2023, 153-155)
BabLBSch16	BM 40396 (Heinrich forthcoming)[191]
BabLBQuo1	BM 40837 (Jiménez and Schmidtchen 2017)
BabLBQuo2	BM 92705 (Frahm, Frazer and Jiménez 2013, with further references)
SIPPAR	
SipNB1	IM 124633 (George and Al-Rawi 1998, 202-203)
SipNB2	IM 132673 (Fadhil and Jiménez forthcoming)
SipNB3a	Si.15 (Schollmeyer 1952-53, pl. 7, 8; *BWL*, pls. 33, 36)
SipNB3b	Si.832 (*CTL* 1, no. 130)
SipNB3c	Si.983 (Adalı forthcoming)
SipNB4a	BM 65472 + BM 76294 + BM 82985 (*CTL* 1, no. 128)
SipNB4b	BM 74197 (*CTL* 1, no. 129)
SipNBQuo1	BM 66965 + BM 76508 (Jiménez 2016)
SipNBSch1	BM 65461 + 1883,0118.2116 (*CTL* 1, no. 141; *BWL* pl. 75; Lambert 2013, pl. 16)
SipNBSch2	BM 55080 + BM 54856[192] (Rozzi 2021b, 219-220; George and Bongenaar 2002, 75)
SipNBSch3	BM 55181 (Rozzi 2022b, 155-157; George and Bongenaar 2002, 75)
URUK	
UrkLB1	IM 135964 (Hunger 1972, 79-89)

[191] Identification by E. Jiménez.

[192] Recently joined to BM 55080 by E. Jiménez and identified as a manuscript of the Šamaš Hymn by Zs. Földi.

Abbreviations and Symbols

Bibliographical Abbreviations

AfO	Archiv für Orientforschung
AHw	W. von Soden, *Akkadisches Handwörterbuch* (1965-1981)
AJSL	The American Journal of Semitic Languages and Literatures
ALA 2	see Pedersén 1986
ALAC	Ancient Languages and Civilizations
AMD	Ancient Magic and Divination
AnOr	Analecta Orientalia
AOAT	Alter Orient und Altes Testament
ARET	Archivi Reali di Ebla, Testi
ASJ	Acta Sumerologica Japonica
ATS	Ancient Textiles Series
AuOrS	Aula Orientalis Supplement
BiOr	Bibliotheca Orientalis
BM	tablets in the collections of the British Museum
BWL	see Lambert 1960a
CAD	*The Assyrian Dictionary of the Oriental Institute of the University of Chicago* (Chicago 1956-2011)
CCP	Cuneiform Commentaries Project (https://ccp.yale.edu/)
CDOG	Colloquien der Deutschen Orient-Gesellschaft
CHANE	Culture and History of the Ancient Near East
CM	Cuneiform Monographs
CMAwR	see Abusch and Schwemer (Luukko and Van Buylaere) 2011, 2016, 2020
CT	Cuneiform Texts from Babylonian Tablets in the British Museum
CTH	see Laroche 1971
CTL	see George and Taniguchi 2019
CTN	Cuneiform Texts from Nimrud
CUSAS	Cornell University Studies in Assyriology and Sumerology
DAAM	Documenta Antiqua Asiae Minoris
DT	tablets in the collections of the British Museum
eBL	electronic Babylonian Library (https://www.ebl.lmu.de/)
eSAD	The Electronic Supplement to the Akkadian Dictionaries (https://www.gkr.uni-leipzig.de/altorientalisches-institut/forschung/supplement-to-the-akkadian-dictionaries)
FAOS	Freiburger Altorientalische Studien
FM	Florilegium Marianum

GAG	W. F. von Soden, *Grundriss der akkadischen Grammatik* (Analalecta Orientalia 33), 3rd edn., with collaboration of W. R. Mayer (Rome 1995)
GBAO	Göttinger Beiträge zum Alten Orient
GMTR	Guides to the Mesopotamian Textual Record
IM	tablets in the collections of the Iraq Museum, Baghdad
ISHR	International Studies in the History of Rhetoric
JANES	Journal of the Ancient Near Eastern Society
JAOS	Journal of the American Oriental Society
JCS	Journal of Cuneiform Studies
JEOL	Jaarbericht van het Vooraziatisch-Egyptisch Genootschap Ex Oriente Lux
JNES	Journal of Near Eastern Studies
JSOTSup	Journal for the Study of the Old Testament. Supplement Series
K	tablets in the collections of the British Museum
KAL	Keilschrifttexte aus Assur literarischen Inhalts
KAR	see Ebeling 1915-1919, 1920-1923
KBo	Keilschrifttexte aus Boghazköi
KUB	Keilschrifturkunden aus Boghazköi
LAOS	Leipziger Altorientalistische Studien
LAPO	Littératures anciennes du Proche-Orient
MC	Mesopotamian Civilizations
MNS	Mnemosyne Supplements
MSL	Materials for the Sumerian Lexicon
NABU	Nouvelles Assyriologiques Brèves et Utilitaires
OBO	Orbis Biblicus et Orientalis
OPSNKF	Occasional Publications of the Samuel Noah Kramer Fund
ORA	Orientalische Religionen in der Antike
OrNS	Orientalia. Nova Series
PIHANS	Publications de l'Institut historique-archéologique néerlandais de Stamboul
QuadSem.	Quaderni di Semitistica
RA	Revue d'Assyriologie et archéologie orientale
RINAP	Royal Inscriptions of the Neo-Assyrian Period
RlA	Reallexikon der Assyriologie und vorderasiatischen Archäologie
SAA	State Archives of Assyria
SAAB	State Archives of Assyria Bulletin
SAACT	State Archives of Assyria Cuneiform Texts
SAAS	State Archives of Assyria Studies
SANER	Studies in Ancient Near Eastern Records
SBLWAW	Society of Biblical Literature Writings from the Ancient World
SFSMD	Studia Francisci Scholten Memoriae Dicata
SGKA	Studien zur Geschichte und Kultur des Altertums
Si	field numbers of tablets excavated at Sippar in the collections of the Archaeological Museums (Istanbul)
Sm	tablets in the collections of the British Museum

SMEA	Studi Micenei ed Egeo-Anatolici
STAC	Studien und Texte zu Antike und Christentum
StBoT	Studien zu den Boğazköy-Texten
StPohl, SM	Studia Pohl, Series Maior
TMH	Texte und Materialien der Frau Professor Hilprecht Collection of Babylonian Antiquits im Eigentum der Universität Jena
TUAT NF	Texte aus der Umwelt des Alten Testaments, Neue Folge
VAT	Vorderasiatisches Museum: Texte
WdO	Welt des Orients
WVDOG	Wissenschaftliche Veröffentlichungen der Deutschen Orient-Gesellschaft
WZKM	Wiener Zeitschrift für die Kunde des Morgenlandes
YBC	siglum of tablets in the Yale Babylonian Collection
ZA	Zeitschrift für Assyriologie

Other Abbreviations and Symbols

cf.	compare
col.	column
e.g.	for example
ibid.	the same as above
l., ll.	line(s)
LB	Late Babylonian
loc. cit.	in the place cited
MA	Middle Assyrian
ms, MS	manuscript
NA	Neo-Assyrian
NB	Neo-Babylonian
OB	Old Babylonian
obv.	obverse
pl.	plate
rev.	reverse
SB	Standard Babylonian
!	collation
?	uncertain reading
x	broken or undeciphered sign
( )	supplied word or sign
⌜ ⌝	a damaged sign or signs
[…]	minor break (one or two missing words)
[……]	major break
…	untranslatable word
……	untranslatable passage

Bibliography

Abrams, M. H. and G. G. Harpham. [8]2005. *A Glossary of Literary Terms* (International student ed.), Boston.

Abusch, T. and D. Schwemer. 2011. *Corpus of Mesopotamian Anti-Witchcraft Rituals. Volume One* (AMD 8/1), Leiden.

Abusch, T., D. Schwemer, M. Luukko and G. Van Buylaere. 2016, 2020. *Corpus of Mesopotamian Anti-Witchcraft Rituals. Volume Two* and *Three* (AMD 8/2-3), Leiden.

Akujärvi, J. 2012. "Pausanias", in I. J. F. de Jong (ed.), *Space in Ancient Greek Literature. Studies in Ancient Greek Narrative* (MNS 33), Leiden - Boston, 235-356.

Alaura, S. and M. Bonechi. 2012. "Il carro del dio del sole nei testi cuneiformi dell'età del Bronzo", SMEA 54, 5-115.

Alster, B. 2007. *Sumerian Proverbs in the Schøyen Collection* (CUSAS 2), Bethesda, MD.

Alster, B. and U. Jeyes. 1990. "Two Hymns and a Copy of a Royal Inscription", ASJ 12, 1-14.

Annus, A. and A. Lenzi. 2010. *Ludlul Bēl Nēmeqi: The Standard Babylonian Poem of the Righteous Sufferer* (SAACT 7), Helsinki.

Arbøll, T. P. 2023. *The Cuneiform Texts from the Danish Excavations of Ḥamā in Syria (1931-1938): Letters, Administrative Documents, Scholarly Texts, Inscriptions, and Seals* (Scientia Danica, Series H, Humanistica, 4, 11), Copenhagen.

Arnaud, D. 2007. *Corpus des textes de bibliothèque de Ras Shamra-Ougarit (1936-2000) en sumérien, babylonien et assyrien* (AuOrS 23), Barcelona.

Bach, J. 2021. "An Analytical Catalogue of Similes and Literal Comparisons in Pre-Neo-Assyrian Royal Narrative Texts", SAAB 27, 1-75.

Baragli, B. 2022a. *Sonnengrüße. Die sumerischen Kiutu-Gebetsbeschwörungen* (AMD 19), Leiden - Boston.

—— 2022b. "The Sun of Nippur: Tracing the Origin of Old Babylonian Sumerian Compositions Utu Based on Literary Features", WZKM 112, 321-346.

—— 2023. "Representing Time in the Kiutu Incantation-Prayers", in S. Helle and G. Konstantopoulos (eds.), *The Shape of Stories: Narrative Structures in Cuneiform Literature* (CM 54), Leiden - Boston, 185-207.

Bawanypeck, D. 2014. "Normative Structures in Mesopotamian Rituals: A Comparison of Hand-lifting Rituals in the Second and First Millennium BC", in D. Bawanypeck and A. Imhausen (eds.), *Traditions of Written Knowledge in Ancient Egypt and Mesopotamia. Proceedings of Two Workshops Held at Goethe-University, Frankfurt/Main in December 2011 and May 2012*, Münster, 71-90.

Beaulieu, P.-A. 2007. "The Social and Intellectual Setting of Babylonian Wisdom Literature", In R. J. Clifford (ed.), *Wisdom Literature in Mesopotamia and Israel,* Atlanta, 3-19.

—— 2022. "Mesopotamian Wisdom", in S. Millar, A. Keefer, and K. Dell (eds.), *The Cambridge Companion to Biblical Wisdom Literature*, Cambridge, 366-388.

Bennett, E. A. 2021. *The Meaning of Sacred Names and Babylonian Scholarship: The Gula Hymn and Other Works* (dubsar 25), Münster.

—— forthcoming (2025). "New Manuscripts of the *Syncretistic Hymn to Gula* (2)", *KASKAL* NS 2.

Berlin, A. 1979. *Enmerkar and Ensuḫkešdanna: A Sumerian Narrative Poem.* (OPSNKF 2), Philadelphia.

—— 1992. "Parallelism", in D.N Freedman (ed.), *The Anchor Yale Bible Dictionary* 5, New York, 154-162.

Black, J. A. and A. Green. 1992/^{2}1998. *Gods, Demons and Symbols of Ancient Mesopotamia. An Illustrated Dictionary*. London.

Böhl, F. M. T. 1942. "De Zonnegod als de Beschermer der Nooddruftigen", JEOL 8, 665-680.

Bonechi, M. 2024. "The join of ARET III 347 with ARET V 6+ and the missing text of the incipit of the Ebla manuscript of the *Hymn to Shamash of Sippar*", in E. Cianfanelli and F. Gori (eds.), *níĝ-ba dub-sar maḫ Studies on Ebla and the Ancient Near East presented to Amalia Catagnoti*, Rome, 77-92.

Borger, R. 1964. Review of Lambert, *Babylonian Wisdom Literature,* JCS 18, 49-56.

—— 1996. *Beiträge zum Inschriftenwerk Assurbanipals. Die Prismenklassen A, B, C = K, D, E, F, G, H, J und T sowie andere Inschriften*, Wiesbaden.

Brünnow, R. E. 1889. "Assyrian Hymns", ZA 4, 1-40; 225-258.

Castellino, G. R. 1976. "The Šamaš Hymn: A Note on Its Structure", in B. L. Eichler, J. W. Heimendinger and Å. W. Sjöberg (eds.), *Kramer Anniversary Volume: Cuneiform Studies in Honor of S. N. Kramer* (AOAT 25), Kevelaer – Neukirchen-Vluyn, 71-74.

—— 1977. *Testi Sumerici e Accadici*, Turin.

Cohen, Y. 2013. *Wisdom from the Late Bronze Age* (SBLWAW 34), Atlanta, GA.

Cohen, Y. and N. Wasserman. 2021. "Mesopotamian Wisdom Literature", in W. Kynes (ed.), *The Oxford Handbook of Wisdom and the Bible*, Oxford, 122-140.

Cuddon, J. A.1991/^{3}1998. *The Penguin Dictionary of Literary Terms and Literary Theory*, New York.

Dalley, S. 1986. "The God Ṣalmu and the Winged Disk", *Iraq* 48, 85-101.

Debourse, C. 2022. *Of Priests and Kings: The Babylonian New Year Festival in the Last Age of Cuneiform Culture* (CHANE 127), Leiden.

De Graef, K. 2014. "All Wool and a Yard Wide. Wool Production and Trade in Old Babylonian Sippar", in C. Breniquet and C. Michel (eds.), *Wool Economy in the Ancient Near East and the Aegean. From the Beginnings of Sheep Husbandry to Institutional Textile Industry* (ATS 17), Oxford - Philadelphia, 202-231.

De Jong, I. J. F. 2012. *Space in Ancient Greek Literature. Studies in Ancient Greek Narrative* (MNS 33), Leiden - Boston.

—— 2014. *Narratology and Classics: A Practical Guide*, Oxford.

Deller, K., W. R. Mayer and W. Sommerfeld. 1987. "Akkadische Lexikographie [Review of CAD N]", OrNS 56, 176-218.

Delnero, P. 2012. "Memorization and the Transmission of Sumerian Literary Compositions", JANES 71, 189-208.

—— 2020. *How to Do Things with Tears: Ritual Lamenting in Ancient Mesopotamia* (SANER 26), Berlin - Boston.

de Ridder, J. J. 2017. "Regional Differences in Middle Assyrian", in O. Drewnowska and M. Sandowicz (eds.), *Fortune and Misfortune in the Ancient Near East. Proceedings of the 60th Rencontre Assyriologique Internationale at Warsaw 21–25 July 2014*, Winona Lake, IN, 297-306.

—— 2018. *Descriptive Grammar of Middle Assyrian* (LAOS 8), Wiesbaden.

De Zorzi, N. 2019. "Literature as Scholarship: Some Reflections on Repetition with Variation and the Construction of Meaning in the Šamaš Hymn 112–117", *KASKAL* 16, 159-182.

—— 2022. "Parallelism and Analogical Thought in Babylonian Poetry: Case Studies from *Ludlul bēl nēmeqi*, the *Babylonian Theodicy*, and the *Šamaš Hymn*", WZKM 112, 367-394.

Donald, T. 1966. "Parallelism in Akkadian, Hebrew and Ugaritic." Unpublished dissertation, University of Manchester.

Ebeling, E. 1915-1919, 1920-1923. *Keilschrifttexte aus Assur religiösen Inhalts*, vols. I-II (WVDOG 28 and 34), Leipzig.

—— 1954. "Ein Hymnus auf die Suprematie des Sonnengottes in Exemplaren aus Assur und Boghazköi", OrNS 23, 209-216.

Engels, J. 2013. "Ringkomposition", in G. Ueding (ed.), *Historisches Wörterbuch der Rhetorik Online*, Berlin - Boston, https://doi.org/10.1515/hwro.8.ringkomposition

Fadhil, A. A. and E. Jiménez. 2019. "Literary Texts from the Sippar Library I: Two Babylonian Classics", ZA 109, 155-176.

—— 2022. "Literary Texts from the Sippar Library III: 'Eriš šummi', a Syncretistic Hymn to Marduk", ZA 112, 229-274.

—— 2023. "Literary Texts from the Sippar Library IV: A 'Macranthropic' Hymn to Ninurta", ZA 113, 193-222.

—— 2024. "Literary Texts from the Sippar Library V: A Hymn in Praise of Babylon and the Babylonians", *Iraq* 86, 1-58.

Faulkner, A. and O. Hodkinson. 2015. *Hymnic Narrative and the Narratology of Greek Hymns* (MNS 384), Leiden - Boston.

Földi, Z. J. 2021a. "A Syncretistic Hymn to Ištar", with contributions by A. C. Heinrich, E. Jiménez and T. D. N. Mitto. Translated by Wilfred G. Lambert, *electronic Babylonian Library*, https://doi.org/10.5282/ebl/l/3/8.

—— 2021b. "Hymn to the Queen of Nippur", with contributions by A.C. Heinrich, A. Hätinen, E. Jiménez and T. D. N. Mitto. Translated by Benjamin R. Foster. *electronic Babylonian Library*, https://doi.org/10.5282/ebl/l/3/6.

—— 2022a. "Counsels of Wisdom", with contributions by A. C. Heinrich, E. Jiménez and T. D. N. Mitto. Translated by Benjamin R. Foster, *electronic Babylonian Library*, https://doi.org/10.5282/ebl/l/2/3.

—— 2022b. "*Bullussa-rabi's Hymn to Gula* as Part of a Series", *KASKAL* 19, 167-168.

—— forthcoming (2025). "*Bullussa-rabi's Hymn to Gula*: More of MS b", *KASKAL* NS 2.

Foster, B. R. 1993/[3]2005. *Before the Muses: An Anthology of Akkadian Literature*, Bethesda.

—— 2007. *Akkadian Literature of the Late Period* (GMTR 2), Münster.

Foster, B. R. and A. R. George. 2020. "An Old Babylonian Dialogue between a Father and his Son", ZA 110, 37-61.

Frahm, E. 2009. "Warum die Brüder Böses planten. Überlegungen zu einer alten Crux in Asarhaddons 'Ninive A'-Inschrift", in W. Arnold, M. Jursa, W. W. Müller, and S. Procházka (eds.), *Philologisches und Historisches zwischen Anatolien und Sokotra: Analecta Semitica in Memoriam Alexander Sima*, Leipzig, 27-49.

Frahm, E., M. Frazer and E. Jiménez. 2013. "Commentary on *Iqqur īpuš*, série mensuelle (*Ayyāru*) (CCP 3.8.2.B)", Cuneiform Commentaries Project (E. Frahm, E. Jiménez, M. Frazer, and K. Wagensonner), 2013-2024, https://ccp.yale.edu/P461300. DOI: 10079/5qfttst [accessed August 26, 2024]

—— 2016. "Commentary on Sagig 4 (CCP 4.1.4.C)", Cuneiform Commentaries Project (E. Frahm, E. Jiménez, M. Frazer, and K. Wagensonner), 2013-2024; accessed August 26, 2024, at https://ccp.yale.edu/P461193. DOI: 10079/ngf1vwj

Frame, G. and A. R. George. 2005. "The Royal Libraries of Nineveh: New Evidence for King Ashurbanipal's Tablet Collecting", *Iraq* 67, 265-284.

Frankena, R. 1962. Review of Lambert, *Babylonian Wisdom Literature*, BiOr 19, 162-165.

Furley, W. D. and J. M. Bremer. 2001. *Greek Hymns: Selected Cult Songs from the Archaic to the Hellenistic Period, I* (STAC 1), Tübingen.

Gabbay, U. 2013. "The Performance of Emesal Prayers Within the Regular Temple Cult of Ancient Mesopotamia: Content and Ritual Setting", in K. Kaniuth et al. (eds.), *Tempel im Alten Orient* (CDOG 7), Wiesbaden, 103-121.

Garfinkle, S. J. 2010. "Merchants and State Formation in Early Mesopotamia", in S. C. Melville and A. L. Slotsky (eds.), *Opening the Tablet Box. Near Eastern Studies in Honor of Benjamin R. Foster* (CHANE 42), Leiden, 185-202.

Geller, M. J. 1997. "The Last Wedge", ZA 87, 43-95.

Genette, G. 1988. *Narrative Discourse Revisited*, Ithaca, NY.

George, A. R. 2003. *The Babylonian Gilgamesh Epic: Introduction, Critical Edition, and Cuneiform Texts*, Oxford.

—— 2007. "The Epic of Gilgamesh: Thoughts on Genre and Meaning", in J. Azize and N. Weeks (eds.), *Gilgamesh and the World of Assyria: Proceedings of the Conference Held at the Mandelbaum House, the University of Sydney (21-23 July 2004)*, Leuven, 37-66.

George, A. R. and F. N. H. Al-Rawi. 1998. "Tablets from the Sippar Library VII - Three Wisdom Texts", *Iraq* 60, 187-206.

George, A. R. and A. C. V. M. Bongenaar. 2002. "Tablets from Sippar: Supplementary bibliography etc. for Leichty, Catalogues VI-VIII, up to the end of 2000", OrNS 71, 55-156.

George, A. R. and J. Taniguchi. 2019. *Cuneiform Texts from the Folios of W. G. Lambert. Part One* (MC 24), Winona Lake, IN.

Gesche, P. D. 2001. *Schulunterricht in Babylonien im 1. Jahrtausend v.Chr.* (AOAT 275), Münster.

Giusfredi, F., V. Pisaniello and A. Matessi. 2023. *Contacts of Languages and Peoples in the Hittite and Post-Hittite World* (ALAC 4), Leiden.

Gray, C. D. 1901a. "A Hymn to Šamaš", AJSL 17(3), 129-145.

—— 1901b. *The Šamaš Religious Texts Classified in the British Museum Catalogue as Hymns, Prayers and Incantations*, Chicago.

Groneberg, B. 1987. *Syntax, Morphologie und Stil der jungbabylonischen "hymnischen" Literatur* (FAOS 14/1-2), Stuttgart.

Guichard, M. 2014. *L' épopée de Zimrī-Lîm* (FM 14. Mémoires de NABU 16), Paris.

Harris, R. 1975. *Ancient Sippar. A Demographic Study of an Old-Babylonian City (1894-1595 B.C.)* (PIHANS 36), Leiden.

Hätinen, A. 2022. "Righteous Sufferer (*Ludlul bēl nēmeqi*) Chapter I-V", with contributions by Z. J. Földi, A. C. Heinrich, E. Jiménez and T. D. N. Mitto. Translated by Benjamin R. Foster, *electronic Babylonian Library*, https://doi.org/10.5282/ebl/l/2/2.

Hecker, K. 2013. "Akkadische Hymnen und Gebete", in B. Janowski and D. Schwemer (eds.), *Hymnen, Klagelieder und Gebete* (TUAT NF 7), Gütersloh, 51-98.

Heimpel, W. 1986. "The Sun at Night and the Doors of Heaven in Babylonian Texts", JCS 38, 127-151.

Heinrich, A. C. Forthcoming. "New Manuscripts and Fragments of the Babylonian Epic of Creation (Enūma eliš) – Part 2", *KASKAL NS* 2.

Heinrich, A. C. and E. Jiménez. 2021. "Ninurta Lore in Neo-Babylonian Nippur: Two Exercise Tablets with Excerpts from Lugale, Angim, and Anzû", *KASKAL* 18, 163-169.

Helle, S. 2014. "Rhythm and Expression in Akkadian Poetry", ZA 104, 56-73.

Hess, C. W. 2010. "Towards the Origins of the Hymnic Epic Dialect", *KASKAL* 7, 101-22.

—— 2015. "Songs of Clay: Materiality and Poetics in Early Akkadian Epic", in P. Delnero and J. Lauinger (eds.), *Texts and Contexts: The Circulation and Transmission of Cuneiform Texts in Social Space* (SANER 9), Berlin, 251-284.

Horowitz, W. 1990. "Two Notes on Etana's Flight to Heaven", OrNS 59, 511-517, pl. 90.

—— 1998. *Mesopotamian Cosmic Geography* (MC 8), Winona Lake, IN.

Hrůša, I. 2015. *Ancient Mesopotamian Religion: A Descriptive Introduction*, Münster.

Hühn, P. et al. (eds.). 2013. *The Living Handbook of Narratology*, http://www.lhn.uni-hamburg.de/. Hamburg.

Hunger, H. 1968. *Babylonische und assyrische Kolophone* (AOAT 2), Neukirchen-Vluyn.

—— 1972. "Die Tontafelfunde der XXVII. Kampagne", Uruk Vorläufiger Bericht 26/27, 79-89.

Hurowitz, V. A. 2007. "An Allusion to the Šamaš Hymn in The Dialogue of Pessimism", in R. J. Clifford (ed.), *Wisdom Literature in Mesopotamia and Israel*, Atlanta, 33-36.

Hyatt, J. P. 1941. *The Treatment of Final Vowels in Early Neo-Babylonian*, New Haven, CT.

Jiménez, E. 2016. "Commentary on Sagig 4 (CCP 4.1.4.B)", in E. Frahm, E. Jiménez, et al. *Cuneiform Commentaries* Project (2013-2024), https://ccp.yale.edu/P285998. DOI: 10079/7h44jcv.

—— 2017a. *The Babylonian Disputation Poems: With Editions of the Series of the Poplar, Palm, and Vine, the Series of the Spider, and the Story of the Poor, Forlorn Wren* (CHANE 87), Leiden.

—— 2017b. "Commentary on Literary Prayer to Marduk2 (CCP 1.5)", in E. Frahm et al., *Cuneiform Commentaries Project*, https://ccp.yale.edu/P461258. DOI: 10079/d51c5pv.

—— 2018. "An Almost Irresistible Target. Parodying the Theodicy in Babylonian Literature", in T. Oshima (ed.), *Teaching Morality in Antiquity: Wisdom Texts, Oral Traditions, and Images* (ORA 29), Tübingen, 124-134.

—— 2022. *Middle and Neo-Babylonian Literary Texts in the Frau Professor Hilprecht Collection* (TMH 13), Jena.

Jiménez, E. and E. Schmidtchen. 2017. "Explaining Diagnosis. Two New Commentaries on the Diagnostic Series *Sagig*", WdO 47, 216-241.

Jursa, M. 1999. "Der Schreiber des Sippar-Manuskripts der Šamaš-Hymne", NABU 1999/104, 101.

—— 2015. "Late Babylonian Epigraphy: A Case Study", in E. Devecchi, G. G. W. Müller and J. Mynářová (eds.), *Current Research in Cuneiform Palaeography. Proceedings of the Workshop organised at the 60th Rencontre Assyriologique Internationale, Warsaw 2014*, Gladbeck, 187-198.

Kalla, G. 2011. "Sippar. A. I. Im 3. und 2. Jahrtausend", RlA 12, 528-533.

Knittel, A. and I. K. Kording. 2013. "Hymne" in G. Ueding (ed.), *Historisches Wörterbuch der Rhetorik Online*, Berlin – Boston, https://doi.org/10.1515/hwro.4.hymne.

Krebernik, M. 1992. "Mesopotamian Myths at Ebla: ARET 5, 6 and ARET 5, 7", in P. Fronzaroli (ed.), *Literature and Literary Language at Ebla* (QuadSem 18), Florence, 41-62.

—— 1998. "Die Texte Aus Fāra Und Tell Abū Ṣalābīḫ", in P. Attinger and M. Wäfler (eds.), *Annäherungen 1: Mesopotamien. Späturuk-Zeit und Frühdynastische Zeit* (OBO 160/1), Freiburg, 235-427.

—— 2009-11. "Sonnengott. A. i. In Mesopotamien. Philologisch", RlA 12, 599-611.

Krebernik, M. and J. J. W. Lisman. 2020. *The Sumerian Zame Hymns from Tell Abū Ṣalābīḫ: With an Appendix on the Early Dynastic Colophons* (dubsar 12), Münster.

Kubiak-Schneider, A. 2022. "Hatra of Shamash. How to assign the city under the divine power?" In C. Bonnet, T. Galoppin et al. (eds.), *Naming and Mapping the Gods in the Ancient Mediterranean: Spaces, Mobilities, Imaginaries*, Berlin - Boston, 791-804.

Kurmangaliev, A. 2009-11. "Sonnengott. B. I. In Mesopotamien. Archäologisch*"*, RlA 12, 616-620.

Lambert, W. G. 1960a. *Babylonian Wisdom Literature*, Oxford.

—— 1960b. "Three Literary Prayers of the Babylonians", AfO 19, 47-66.

—— 1967. "The Gula Hymn of Bullutsa-rabi", OrNS 36, 105-132.

—— 1982. "The Hymn to the Queen of Nippur", in G. Van Driel et al. (eds.), *Zikir Šumim: Assyriological Studies Presented to F. R. Kraus on the Occasion of His Seventieth Birthday* (SFSMD 5), Leiden, 173-218.

—— 2004. "Exiles and Deportees: A Third Category", in C. Nicolle (ed.), *Nomades et sédentaires dans le Proche-Orient ancien. Compte rendu de la XLVIe Rencontre Assyriologique Internationale* (Amurru 3), Paris, 213-217.

—— 2007. *Babylonian Oracle Questions* (MC 13), Winona Lake, IN.

—— 2013. *Babylonian Creation Myths* (MC 16), Winona Lake, IN.

Lambert, W. G. and R. D. Winters (edited by A. R. George and M. Krebernik). 2023. An = Anum *and Related Lists, God Lists of Ancient Mesopotamia I* (ORA 54), Tübingen.

Lanham, R. A. 2014. *Handlist of Rhetorical Terms*. 3rd ed. Berkeley.

Laroche, E. 1971. *Catalogue des textes hittites*, Paris.

Lausberg, H. 1998. *Handbook of Literary Rhetoric: A Foundation for Literary Study*, Leiden.

Leichty, E. (with an introduction by J. E. Reade). 1986. *Catalogue of the Babylonian Tablets in the British Museum Volume VI: Tablets from Sippar 1*, London.

Leichty, E., I. L. Finkel and C. B. F. Walker. 2019. *Catalogue of the Babylonian Tablets in the British Museum*, vols 4-5 (dubsar 10), Münster.

Leichty, E. and A. K. Grayson. 1987. *Catalogue of the Babylonian Tablets in the British Museum. Volume VII: Tablets from Sippar 2*, London.

Lenzi, A. 2018. "Old Babylonian Prayer to Anuna", in A. Lenzi, *Akkadian Prayer Miscellany*, http://akkpm.org/P269974.html

—— 2019. *An Introduction to Akkadian Literature: Contexts and Content*, University Park, PA.

Leonhardt, H. 2024. *Neuassyrische Grammatik* (LAOS 16), Leipzig.

Ludwig, M.-C. and C. Metcalf. 2017. "The Song of Innana and Išme-Dagan: An Edition of BM 23820+23831", ZA 107, 1-21.

Luukko, M. 2004. *Grammatical Variation in Neo-Assyrian* (SAAS 16), Helsinki.

Maul, S. M. 1999. "Gottesdienst im Sonnenheiligtum zu Sippar", in B. Böck, E. Cancik-Kirschbaum, and T. Richter (eds.), *Munuscula Mesopotamica: Festschrift für Johannes Renger* (AOAT 267), Münster, 285-316.

Maul, S. M. and S. Manasterska. 2023. *Schreiberübungen aus neuassyrischer Zeit* (KAL 15/WVDOG 162), Wiesbaden.

Mayer, W. R. 1976. *Untersuchungen zur Formensprache der babylonischen "Gebetsbeschwörungen"*(StPohl, SM 5), Rome.

—— 1988. "Ein neues Königsritual gegen feindliche Bedrohung", OrNS 57, 145-164.
—— 1992a. "Das gnomische Präteritum im literarischen Akkadisch", in OrNS 61, 373-399.
—— 1992b. "Ein Hymnus auf Ninurta als Helfer in der Not", OrNS 61, 17-57.
—— 1995. "Zum Terminativ-Adverbialis im Akkadischen. Die Modaladverbien auf *-iš*", OrNS 64, 161-186.
—— 1996. "Zum Pseudo-Lokativadverbialis im Jungbabylonischen", OrNS 65, 428-434.
—— 2003. "Akkadische Lexikographie [Review of CAD R]", OrNS 72, 231-242.
—— 2017. "Zum akkadischen Wörterbuch: M-S", OrNS 86, 1-41.
Metcalf, C. 2011. "New Parallels in Hittite and Sumerian Praise of the Sun", WdO 41, 168-176.
—— 2015a. "Old Babylonian Religious Poetry in Anatolia: From Solar Hymn to Plague Prayer", ZA 105, 42-53.
—— 2015b. *The Gods Rich in Praise: Early Greek and Mesopotamian Religious Poetry*, Oxford.
—— 2023. "The New Akkadian Solar Hymn and Prayer from Ortaköy/Šapinuwa (DAAM 2.6): An Interpretation and Trilingual Commentary", WdO 53(1), 46-75.
Metzler, K. A. 2002. *Tempora in altbabylonischen literarischen Texten* (AOAT 279), Münster.
Michalowski, P. 1996. "Ancient Poetics", in E. Vogelzang and H. L. J. Vanstiphout (eds.), *Mesopotamian Poetic Language: Sumerian and Akkadian* (CM 6), Groningen, 141-153.
Nakata, I. 1970-71. "Mesopotamian Merchants and their Ethos", JANES 3, 90-101.
Norden, E. 1956. *Agnostos Theos: Untersuchungen zur Formengeschichte religiöser Rede*, Leipzig - Berlin.
Novotny, J. R. and J. Jeffers. 2018. *The Royal Inscriptions of Ashurbanipal (668-631 BC), Assur-etel-ilāni (630-627 BC), and Sîn-šarra-iškun (626-612 BC), Kings of Assyria* (RINAP 5/1), University Park, PA.
Nurullin, R. 2013. "An Attempt at *Šimâ milka* (Ugaritica V, 163 and Duplicates). Part I: Prologue, Instructions II, III, IV", *Babel und Bibel* 7, 175-229.
Oshima, T. M. 2011. *Babylonian Prayers to Marduk* (ORA 7), Tübingen.
—— 2018. "When the Godless Thrives and a Wolf Grows Fat: Explaining the Prosperity of the Impious in Ancient Mesopotamian Wisdom Texts", in *Teaching Morality in Antiquity. Wisdom Texts, Oral Traditions, and Images* (ORA 29), Tübingen, 189-216.
Pedersén, O. 1986. *Archives and Libraries in the City of Assur: A Survey of the Material from the German Excavations. Part II.* Acta Universitatis Upsaliensis (Studia Semitica Upsaliensia 8), Uppsala.
Piccin, M. 2021. *Linguistic Aspects of Persuasiveness in Akkadian: Petitions and Prayers* (AOAT 446), Münster.
Pirngruber, R. 2019. "Cuneiform Palaeography in First Millennium BC Babylonia", in E. Devecchi, J. Mynářová and G. G. W. Müller (eds.), *Current Research in Cuneiform Palaeography 2. Proceedings of the Workshop*

organised at the 64th Rencontre Assyriologique Internationale, Innsbruck 2018, Gladbeck, 157-175.

Plett, H. F. 2010. *Literary Rhetoric: Concepts – Structures – Analyses* (ISHR 2), Leiden.

Pohl, A. 2022. *Die akkadischen Hymnen der altbabylonischen Zeit: Grammatik, Stilistik, Editionen* (LAOS 13), Leipzig.

Polonsky, J. 2002. "The Rise of the Sun God and the Determination of Destiny in Ancient Mesopotamia." PhD Dissertation, University of Philadelphia.

Reade, J. E. 2000. "Ninive (Niniveh)", RlA 9, 388-433.

Reiner, E. 1985. *Your Thwarts in Pieces, Your Mooring Rope Cut. Poetry from Babylonia and Assyria* (Michigan Studies in the Humanities 5), Ann Arbor, MI.

—— 1991. "First-Millennium Babylonian Literature", in I. E. S. Boardman et al. (eds.), *The Assyrian and Babylonian Empires and Other States of the Near East, from the Eighth to the Sixth Centuries B.C., The Cambridge Ancient History Second Edition* 3/2, Cambridge, 293-321.

Richardson, N. 2015. *Constructing a Hymnic Narrative: Tradition and Innovation in the Longer Homeric Hymns*, in A. Faulkner and O. Hodkinson (eds.), *Hymnic Narrative and the Narratology of Greek Hymns* (MNS 384), Leiden - Boston, 19-30.

Rieken, E., J. Lorenz and A. Daues. 2017. *Gebete der Hethiter*. www.hethiter.net/txhetgebet.

Rowton, M. B. 1962. "The Use of the Permansive in Classic Babylonian", JNES 21, 233-303.

Rozzi, G. 2021a. "Great Prayer to Šamaš", with contributions by A. C. Heinrich, E. Jiménez, and T. D. N. Mitto. Translated by Benjamin R. Foster. *Electronic Babylonian Library*, https://doi.org/10.5282/ebl/l/3/4

—— 2021b. "New Manuscripts of the Great Šamaš Hymn", *KASKAL* 18, 213-222.

—— 2022a. "Great Prayer to Nabû", with contributions by A. C. Heinrich, A. Hätinen, E. Jiménez, and T. D. N. Mitto. Translated by Benjamin R. Foster. *Electronic Babylonian Library*, https://doi.org/10.5282/ebl/l/3/5

—— 2022b. "New Manuscripts of the Great Šamaš Hymn (2)", *KASKAL* 19 151-157.

—— 2023. "New Manuscripts of the Great Šamaš Hymn (3)", *KASKAL* 20, 153-156.

—— 2024a. *The Akkadian Great Hymns and Prayers. A Critical Edition of the Nabû and Ištar Prayers and a Study of the Corpus* (Antichistica 42 / Studi Orientali 15), Venice.

—— 2024b. "How to Write a Hymn: Material Features in Manuscripts of Akkadian Poetry", *KASKAL* NS 1, 323-340.

Scheil, V. 1902. *Une saison de fouilles à Sippar*, Cairo.

Schollmeyer, A. 1912. *Sumerisch-Babylonische Hymnen und Gebete an Šamaš* (SGKA Ergänzungsband 1), Paderborn.

Schollmeyer, F. 1952-1953. "Ein neubabylonisches Duplikat zu dem Šamaš-Hymnus K 3182", AfO 16, 46.

Schwemer, D. 2014. "Form Follows Function? Rhetoric and Poetic Language in First Millennium Akkadian Incantations", WdO 44, 263-288.

—— 2015. "Hittite Prayers to the Sun-God for Appeasing an Angry Personal God", In M. Jaques, *Mon dieu qu'ai-je fait? Les diĝir-šà-dab(5)-ba et la piété privée en Mésopotamie* (OBO 273), Fribourg - Göttingen, 349-393.

—— 2017. *The Anti-Witchcraft Ritual Maqlû: The Cuneiform Sources of a Magic Ceremony from Ancient Mesopotamia*, Wiesbaden.

—— forthcoming. "Cuneiform in Contact: Or, How the Hittites Learned to Pray", in D. Prechel, A. Pruß, T. Richter and D. Wicke (eds.) in collaboration with M. Würz, *Kultur – Kontakt – Kultur, Beiträge anlässlich der 66. Rencontre Assyriologique Internationale in Frankfurt/Main und Mainz, 25.–29. Juli 2022* (dubsar 35), Münster.

Schwemer, D. and A. Süel. 2021. *The Akkadian and Sumerian Texts from Ortaköy-Šapinuwa* (DAAM 2), Leipzig.

Seidl, U. 2020. "The Winged Disc in Mesopotamia", in A. Otto, M. Herles and K. Kaniuth (eds.), *Proceedings of the 11th International Congress on the Archaeology of the Ancient Near East. Volume 1*, Wiesbaden, 119-150.

Setälä, A. 2022. "Descent of Ištar (Chapter: Standard Babylonian)", with contributions by Z. J. Földi, A. Hätinen, E. Jiménez and G. Rozzi. Translated by Benjamin R. Foster. *Electronic Babylonian Library*, https://doi.org/10.5282/ebl/l/1/8.

Seux, M.-J. 1976. *Hymnes et prières aux dieux de Babylonie et d'Assyrie* (LAPO 8), Paris.

Shehata, D. 2009. *Musiker und ihr vokales Repertoire: Untersuchungen zu Inhalt und Organisation von Musikerberufen und Liedgattungen in altbabylonischer Zeit* (GBAO 3), Göttingen.

Shibata, D. 2008. "A Nimrud Manuscript of the Fourth Tablet of the Series *mīs pî*, *CTN* IV 170 (+) 188, and a *Kiutu* Incantation to the Sun God", *Iraq* 70, 189-204.

Sloane, T. O. 2001. *Encyclopedia of Rhetoric*, Oxford - New York.

Soden, W. von. 1931. "Der hymnisch-epische Dialekt des Akkadischen", ZA 40, 163-227.

—— 1933. "Der hymnisch-epische Dialekt des Akkadischen", ZA 41, 90-183.

—— 1971. "Der Große Hymnus an Nabû", ZA 61, 44-71.

—— 1972-75. "Hymne B. Nach akkadischen Quellen" RlA 4, 544-548.

—— 1977. Review of Seux, *Hymnes et prières*, ZA 67, 279-284.

Soden, W. von and W. Röllig. 1991. *Das akkadische Syllabar* (4. Aufl.) (AnOr 42), Rome.

Sommerfeld, W. 1982. *Der Aufstieg Marduks. Die Stellung Marduks in der babylonischen Religion des zweiten Jahrtausends v. Chr.* (AOAT 213), Kevelaer – Neukirchen-Vluyn.

Starr, I. 1990. *Queries to the Sungod. Divination and Politics in Sargonid Assyria* (SAA 4), Helsinki.

Steinberger, C. Forthcoming (a revised edition of an unpublished dissertation): "Versstruktur und Parallelismus. Untersuchungen zur akkadischen und ugaritischen Poesie der Spätbronzezeit" (Kasion), Münster.

Steinkeller, P. 2005. "Of Stars and Men: The Conceptual and Mythological Setup of Babylonian Extispicy", in A. Gianto (ed.), *Biblical and Oriental Essays in Memory of William L. Moran* (Biblica et Orientalia 48), Rome, 11-47.

Steitler, C. W. 2017. *The Solar Deities of Bronze Age Anatolia: Studies in Texts of the Early Hittite Kingdom* (StBoT 62), Wiesbaden.

Streck, M. P. 2007. "Der Parallelismus Membrorum in den altbabylonischen Hymnen", in A. Wagner (ed.), *Parallelismus Membrorum* (OBO 224), Freiburg - Göttingen, 167-181.

—— 2014. "Die Kasusflexion im Status Rectus des Neu- und Spätbabylonischen", in M. Krebernik and H. Neumann (eds.), *Babylonien und seine Nachbarn in neu- und spätbabylonischer Zeit: Wissenschaftliches Kolloquium aus Anlass des 75. Geburtstags von Joachim Oelsner* (AOAT 369), Münster, 247-288.

—— 2020. "Altbabylonische Hymnen – eine Gattung?" in I. Arkhipov, L. Kogan, and N. Koslova (eds.), *The Third Millennium: Studies in Early Mesopotamia and Syria in Honor of Walter Sommerfeld and Manfred Krebernik* (CM 50), Leiden - Boston, 659-674.

Streck, M. P., N. Rudik, E. Zomer, J. Wende, and N. J. C. Kouwenberg. 2013-. *The Electronic Supplement to the Akkadian Dictionaries (eSAD).* https://altorient.gko.uni-leipzig.de/etymd.html

Thureau-Dangin, F. 1925. "Un hymne à Iśtar de la haute époque babylonienne", RA 22, 169-177.

Veenhof, K. R. 2004. "Trade With the Blessing of Šamaš in Old Babylonian Sippar", in J. G. Dercksen (ed.), *Assyria and Beyond. Studies Presented to Mogens Trolle Larsen* (PIHANS 100), Leiden, 551-582.

Vogelzang, M. E. 1996. "Repetition as a Poetic Device in Akkadian", in M. E. Vogelzang and H. L. J. Vanstiphout (eds.), *Mesopotamian Poetic Language: Sumerian and Akkadian* (CM 6), Groningen, 167-182.

Wagensonner, K. 2020. "YBC 11431, a draft letter or an exercise?" NABU 2020/98, 203-205.

Wasserman, N. 2003. *Style and Form in Old Babylonian Literary Texts* (CM 27), Leiden - Boston.

—— 2020. *The Flood: The Akkadian Sources. A New Edition, Commentary, and a Literary Discussion* (OBO 290), Leuven - Paris - Bristol.

Watson, W. G. E. 1994. *Traditional Techniques in the Classical Hebrew Verse* (JSOTSup 170), Sheffield.

West, M. L. 1997. "Akkadian Poetry: Metre and Performance", *Iraq* 59, 175-187.

Westenholz, J. G. 1999. "In the Shadow of the Muses: A View of Akkadian Literature Before the Muses", JAOS 119, 80-87.

Wilcke, C. 1972-75. "Hymne I", RlA 4, 539-544.

Wisnom, S. 2015. "Stress Patterns in Enūma Eliš: A Comparative Study", *KASKAL* 12, 485-502.

—— 2019. *Weapons of Words: Intertextual Competition in Babylonian Poetry: A Study of* Anzû, Enūma Eliš, *and* Erra and Išum (CHANE 106), Leiden.

Worthington, M. 2012. *Principles of Akkadian Textual Criticism* (SANER 1), Boston - Berlin.

CUNEIFORM TEXT

The Great Hymn to Šamaš

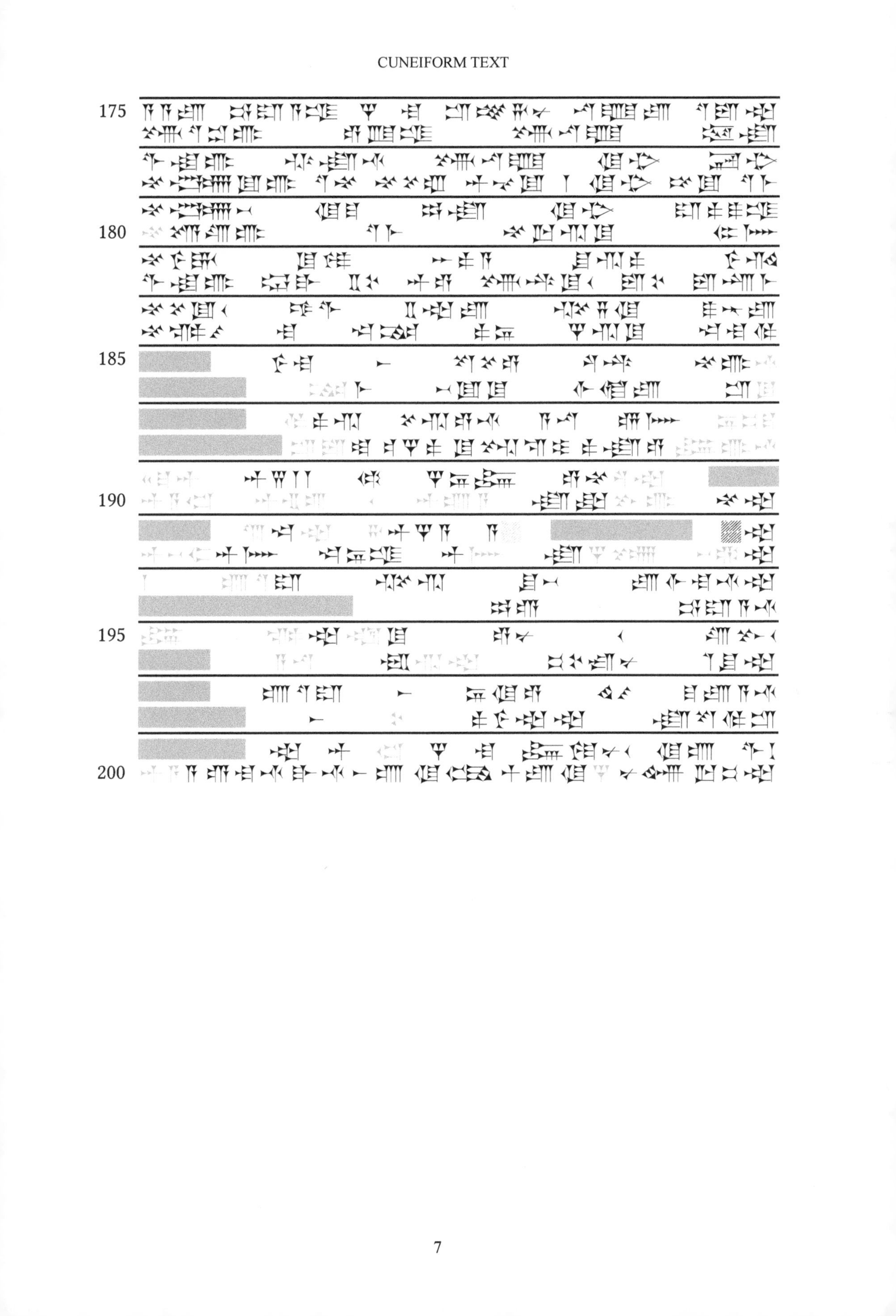

TRANSLITERATION

muš-na-mir *gi-mir* *šá-ma-mi*
mu-šah-li *ek-le-tu*$_4$ *a-na* UN.MEŠ *e-liš u šap-liš*
^{d}UTU *muš-na-mir* *gi-mir* *šá-ma-mi*
mu-šah-li *ek-le-tu*$_4$ *a-na* UN.⸢MEŠ⸣ *e-liš u šap-liš*
sah-pu *ki-ma* *šu-uš-kal-lu* KI-*tì* *šá-ru-ru-ka*
šá *hur-šá-a-ni* *bé-ru-ti* *e-ṭ*[*u-t*]*i-šu-nu* *tuš-par-di*
a-na *ta-mar-ti-ka* *ih-du-ú* DINGIR.MEŠ *u* *ma-al-ku*
i-riš-šu-ka *gi-mir-šú-nu* ^{d}*í-gì-gì*
pu-uz-ru *sat-tak-ku* *šu-hu-zu* *ba-ri-ru-ka*
ina na-mir-ti UD.DA-*ka* *ki-bi-is-si-na* *in-na-*[*mar*]
mé-lam-mu-ka *iš-te-né-ʾu-*⸢*ú*⸣ [*šá-ma-mi*]
kib-rat *er-bet-ti* *ki-ma* ^{d}GIŠ.BA[R *iš-ta-ah-na*]
tuš-pal-ki *ba-a-bi* *šá* *ka-liš* [*pa-rak-ki*]
šá *kul-lat* ^{d}*í-gì-gì* NIDBA.MEŠ-*šú-n*[*u tuš-ta-šir*]
^{d}UTU *ana* *a-ṣi-ka* *kit-mu-sa* *te-né-še-e-ti*
⸢*uš-te-ep*⸣-[*pe-r*]*a* ⸢*a-na* *nu-ri*⸣-[*ka*] *gi-mir-ši-na* KUR.K[UR]
muš-na-mir *pe-tu-u* *ek-le-ti* *ṣer-ret* *šá-m*[*a-mi*]
mu-šah-miṭ *ziq* *šat ur-ri* *me-reš* ŠE-*im* *na-piš-*[*ti*] ⸢KUR⸣
šá-di-i *bé-ru-ti* *e-ri-ma* *šá-lum-mat-ka*
nam-ri-ru-ka *im-lu-ú* *si-hi-ip* KUR.KUR
šu-ra-ta *ana* *hur-sa-a-ni* *er-ṣe-ta* *ta-bar-ri*
kip-pat KUR.KUR *ina qé-reb* AN-*e* *šaq-la-a-ta*
UN.MEŠ KUR.KUR *kul-lat-si-na* *ta-paq-qid*

šá ^{d}*é-a* LUGAL *mal-ku uš-tab-nu-ú ka-liš paq-da-ka*
šu-ut na-piš-ti šak-na mit-ha-riš te-re-ʾe
at-ta-ma na-qid-si-na šá e-liš u šap-liš
te-te-né-ti-iq gi-na-a šá-ma-mi
[š]u-um-dul-ta er-ṣe-tu ta-ba-aʾ u$_4$*-mi-šam*
⸢ILLU⸣ A.AB.BA *hur-sa-a-ni er-ṣe-ta šá-ma-mi*
ki-i ⸢*ták-kàs*⸣*-si gi-na-a ta-ba-aʾ u*$_4$*-mi-šam*
šap-la-a-ti ma-al-ki ^{d}*kù-bu* ^{d}*a-nun-na-ki ta-paq-qid*
e-la-a-ti ša [d]a-ád-me ka-li-ši-na tuš-te-šìr
re-ʾu-u šap-la-a-ti na-qí-du e-la-a-ti
muš-te-šir nu-úr kiš-šá-ti ^{d}UTU *at-ta-ma*
te-te-né-bir ta-ma-tu$_4$ DAGAL-*tu*$_4$ *šá-di-il-ta*
[šá] ^{d}*í-gì-gì la i-du-ú qé-reb lìb-bi-šá*
[^{d}UT]U *bir-bir-ru-ka ina ap-si-i* ⸢*ú-ri*⸣*-du*
[^{d}*lah-m*]*u šu-ut* A.AB.BA *i-na-aṭ-ṭa-lu* ⸢*nu*⸣*-úr-ka*
KUR-⸢*i*⸣ *[k]i-ma qé-e ka-sa-ta ki-ma im-ba-ri [ká]t-ma-ta*
⸢*rap*⸣*-šu an-dùl-la-ka sa-hi-ip* [KU]R.KUR
⸢*ta*⸣*-ta-šu-uš u*$_4$*-me-šam-ma ul iʾ-da-ru pa-n[u]-ka*
⸢*tuš*⸣*-ta-bar-ri ina mu-ši-im-ma tu-šah-miṭ [uk-l]a*
[a]-na šid-di šá la i-de né-su-ti u bé-ri la ma-n[u-ti]
^{d}UTU *dal-pa-ta šá ur-ra tal-li-ka u mu-šá ta-sah-*⸢*ra*⸣
[u]l i-ba-áš-ši ina gi-mir ^{d}*í-gì-gì šá šu-nu-hu ba-li-ka*
[in]a DINGIR.MEŠ *nap-har kiš-šá-ti šá šu-tu-ru ki-ma ka-a-ta*
[ṣ]i-tuk-ka ip-hu-ru DINGIR.MEŠ *ma-a-ti*
[n]a-mur-rat-ka ez-ze-ti ma-a-tu$_4$ *sah-pat*
[š]a$^{?}$ *nap-har* KUR.KUR *šu-ut šu-un-na-a li-šá-nu*
[ti]-i-de kip-di-ši-na ki-bi-is-si-na na-aṭ-la-a-ta

[*kam-s*]*a-nik-ka* *kul-lat-si-na* *te-né-še-e-ti*

[^{d}U]TU *a-na* ZÁLAG-ka *ṣu-um-mu-rat* *mit-har-tu*$_4$

[*a-na*] *ma-kal-ti* *ba-ru-ti* *a-na ri-kis* GIŠ.EREN

[*a-na*] *mu-šem-mi* *šá*-DINGIR.MEŠ *pa-še-ru* MÁŠ.GE$_6$.MEŠ

[*x x*] *x* *šá* *rik-sa-a-ti* *kit-mu-sa* *ma-har-ka*

[*i-na* *ma*]*h-ri-ka* *kit-mu-su* *rag-gu* *u* *ke-e-nù*

[*man*$^{?}$-*nu*$^{?}$] *ur-ra-du* *ina* ABZU *ba-li-ka*

[*šá e*]*b*$^{?}$-*bi* *ki-i-ni* *u* *za-ma-né-e* *tu-šá-pi* *di-in-šu-u*[*n*]

a-rik-tu$_4$ ZI-*tì* *rag-g*[*u* *t*]*u-saq* *u* *tu-š*[*ak-ri*]

i-re-eh-hi-šu-ma šit-⸢*ta* *ki-ma* *ṣa-li*⸣-*li* *i-nap-pu-u*[*š* *ki-i-nu*]

tu-tar-ra *ṣal-pa* *šá* *la-mu-ú* [*e-bir-šu*]

tu-šel-li ina hu-bur šá di-na ti-iṣ-bu-tú [*tu-zak-ka* *din-šu-un*]

ina di-in *ki-na-a-ti* ^{d}UTU *šá* *taq-bu-u-*[*ši-na-ti*]

šu-pu-u *zik-ru-ka* *ul in-nen-nu-u* *pa-na* *ul t*[*u-ub-bal*]

te-em-mi-id *a-na* *al-la-ki* *šá* *šup-šu-qat* *ú-r*[*u-uh-šú*]

a-na e-bir A.AB.BA *a-dir a-ge-e* *ta-nam-di*[*n* *lìb-ba*$^{?}$]

har-ra-na-a-ti *šá* *la* *am-ra* *ṣa-ʾi-da* *ta-š*[*ap-par*]

[*s*]*u-li-i* UŠ.MEŠ-*di* *ma-hi-ru* *šá* ⸢^{d}⸣[UTU]-*ši*

LÚ.DAM.GÀR *na-áš ki-si* *ina* *e-de-e* *tu-še-zib*

tu-šel-li *a-rid* *an-za-nu-un-ze-e* *tu-šá-áš-kan* *kap-pa*

mu-un-nab-tú *mun-nar-bi* *ma-ha-zi* *tu-kal-lam*

har-ra-na-a-ti šá la i-du-ú *tu-kal-lam* *šal-la*

šá *i-na* *pu-uz-ra-at* EDIN ⸢*at*$^{?}$-*ta*$^{?}$⸣ *ta-paṭ-ṭár*

ab-ka šá *ina* É *ṣi-b*[*ít-ti*] *na-du-ú* *tu-kal-lam-šú* *nu-*⸢*ú-ru*⸣

šá DINGIR-*šú* *it-ti-šú* [*ze-nu-ú* *t*]*u-sal-lam*

i-na *a-ma-ri* *te-r*[*e-t*]*i* *uz-na-ši-na* *tuš-pat-ti*

te-mid *a-na* LÚ.GI[G] ⸢*šá* *is-su*$^{?}$-*uh*⸣ *a-dan-šú*

ta-par-ra-as ⸢*ar*⸣-[*ka-a-t*]*ú* *ta-še-ʾe-e* *nap-šá-a-tu*$_4$

tu-ub-bal [*x x x x*]   *ana*   UN.MEŠ-*šú*

ina KUR.NU.GI$_4$.A ⸢KI⸣-[*ti*$^{?}$ *la ta-r*]*i*   *tu-bal-laṭ*   *mi-*⸢*i*⸣*-tu*$_4$

^{d}*iš-tar*.MEŠ   [*š*]*ab-sa-tu*$_4$ *a-na* UN.⸢MEŠ⸣   [*t*]*u-sal-lam*

ṣi-ra-ta-ma ⸢*ul*⸣ *in-nen-na-a*   *qí-bit*   *pi-i-ka*

^{d}UTU   *ina šu-uš-kal-li-ka*   *ha-bi-lu*   ⸢*ta*⸣*-sah-hap*

ina   *giš-par-ri-ka*   *la-pit*   *da-mu*   *ul u-ṣu*

šá a-na ma-mi-ti-ka la i-pal-la-hu   *x* [*x x*   *x x x*]

a-na   *la a-dir*   *za-kir šu-mi-ka*   *da-bi-ba*   *ṣal-*⸢*pa-a*⸣-[*ti*]

tar-ṣa-at   *še-et-ka*   *rap-pu*   *ina* KI-*tì*   *ka-ma-*⸢*ru*$^{?}$⸣-[*ma*$^{?}$]

šá   *a-na*   *al-ti*   *tap-pe-e-šú*   *iš-šu-ú*   *ni-ši*   ⸢*i*$^{?}$⸣-[*ni-šú*$^{?}$]

i-na   *u*$_4$*-um*   *la ši-ma-ti*   *ú-kar*$_5$*-ri*   *mu-ú-*[*tu*]

kun-na-áš-šu   *kip-pu*   *ze-ru*   *ú-kab-ba-*[*as*]

iš-šìr-šú   GIŠ.TUKUL-*ka-ma*   *mu-še-zib*   *ul i-*[*ši*]

ina di-ni-šú   *ul i-za-az-za*   *a-bu-*[*šú*]

ina pi-i   *da-a-a-nu*   *ul ip-pa-lu*   *šu-nu*   ŠEŠ.MEŠ-*šú*

ina   *hu-ha-ri*   *šá*   *e-re-e*   *sa-hi-ip*   *ul*   *i-de*

šá   *ka-ṣir*   *an-zil-li*   *qar-na-šú*   *tu-bal-la*

e-piš   *šid-di*   *ka-pi-du*   *e-ni*   *qaq-qar-šu*

da-a-a-nu   *ṣal-pa*   *mé-se-ra*   *tu-kal-lam*

ma-hir   *ṭa-aʾ-ti*   *la*   *muš-te-še-ru*   *tu-šá-az-bal*   *ar-na*

la ma-hir ṭa-aʾ-ti   *ṣa-bi-tú a-bu-ti*   *en-še*

ṭa-a-bi   UGU ^{d}UTU   TI.LA   *ut-tar*

da-a-a-na   *muš-ta-lu*$_4$ *šá di-in*   *me-šá-ri*   *i-di-nu*

ú-gam-mar   É.GAL   *šu-bat* NUN.MEŠ   *mu-šab-šú*

na-din kàs-pa a-na ṣib-ti   *ha-bi-lu*   *mi-na-a*   *ut-tar*

uš-ta-kaṣ-ṣab a-na né-me-li-ma   *ú-hal-laq*   KUŠ.NÍG.NA$_4$

na-din kàs-pa a-na šid-di SUD.MEŠ   *mu-ter* 1 GÍN *a-na*   *še-*⸢*lal*⸣-[*ti*]

ṭa-a-bi   UGU ^{d}UTU   TI.LA   *ut-*[*tar*]

ṣa-bit zi-ba-ni-ti e-piš ṣi-lip-ti
muš-te-nu-ú NA$_4$ *ki-i-si ú-šaq-qa ú-šap-pal*
uš-ta-kaṣ-ṣa-ab a-na né-me-li-im-ma ú-hal-l[aq ki-i-sa]
šá ki-i-ni ṣa-bit zi-ba-ni-ti ma-aʾ-da [x x]
mim-ma šum-šú ma-aʾ-da qí-šá-áš-šú i-[x x]
ṣa-bit GIŠ.BÁN *e-piš ṣi-l[ip-ti]*
na-din ši-qa-a-ti a-na bi-ri-i mu-šad-din at-ra
ina la u$_4$*-me-šú [a]r-rat* UN.MEŠ *i-kaš-šad-su*
ina la a-dan-ni-šú i[š]-šá-al i-raš-ši bil-ta
NÍG.GA-*šú ul i-be-el* IBILA-*šú*
a-na É-*šú ul ir-ru-bu šu-nu* ŠEŠ.MEŠ-*šú*
um-ma-ni ki-nu na-din ŠE-*im i-na [kab-r]i* PI *ú-šat-tar dum-q[u]*
ṭa-a-ab UGU ^{d}UTU *ba-la-ṭ[u*$^{?}$*] ut-⸢tar⸣*
ú-rap-pa-áš kim-ta meš-ra-a i-ra-áš-š[i]
ki-ma A.MEŠ *nag-bi da-ri-i* NUMUN-[*šú*] *da-[ri]*
a-na e-piš ú-sa-at dum-qí la mu-du-ú [ṣa]-lip-[ti]
muš-ten-nu-ú šap-la-a-ti ina mas-da-ri šá-k[in ina mah-ri-ka]
šu-ut lum-nu i-pu-šú NUMUN-*šú-nu u[l da-ri]*
šu-ut ul-la pi-i-šú-nu šá-kin ina mah-ri-ka
tu-šah-maṭ ṣi-it pi-i-šú-nu ta-pa-áš-šar at-ta
[t]a-šem-me te-bir-ši-na-ti šá rug-gu-gu tu-mas-si di-in-šú
ma-na-ma ma-am-ma pu-uq-qu-du qa-tuk-ka
tuš-te-eš-šir te-re-te-ši-na šá šuk-ṣu-ru ta-paṭ-ṭar
ta-šem-me ^{d}UTU *su-up-pa-a su-la-a ù ka-ra-bu*
šu-ken-na kit-mu-su lit-hu-ša ù la-ban ap-pi
a-na hur-ri pi-i-šú dun-na-mu-ú i-šá-as-si-ka
ú-la-lu en-šú hu-ub-bu-lu muš-ke-nu
um-mi-sal-la mas-da-ra gi-na-a i-mah-har-ka
šá ru-qat kim-ta-šú né-su-ú URU-*ú-šú*

ina šu-ru-bat EDIN *re-ʾu-ú i-mah-har-ka*
ka-par-ri ina te-še-e na-qí-du ina LÚ.KÚR
^{d}UTU *i-mah-har-ka a-lak-tu i-ti-qu pu-luh-ti*
LÚ.DAM.GÀR *al-la-ka* LÚ.ŠÁMAN.LÁ *na-áš* KUŠ.NÍG.NA$_4$
^{d}UTU *i-mah-har-ka* LÚ.ŠU.HA *ka-tim-ti*
ṣa-a-a-du ma-hi-ṣu mu-ter-ru MÁŠ.ANŠE
ina bu-un-zer-ri LÚ.MUŠEN.DÙ *i-mah-har-ka*
mut-tah-li-lu šar-ra-qu mu-ṣal-lu-ú šá ^{d}UTU-*ši*
ina su-le-e EDIN *mut-tag-gi-šú i-mah-har-ka*
mi-i-tu$_4$ mur-tap-pi-du e-ṭém-mu hal-qu
^{d}UTU *im-hu-ru-ka tal-te-me ka-la-ma*
ul tak-li šu-ut im-hu-ru-ka ta-⸢*qiš*!⸣ *ta-din*
a-na ia-a-ti ^{d}UTU *la ta-zer-ši-na-ti*
šá ad-[*na*]*-a-ti* ^{d}UTU GEŠTU.2-*ši-na tuš-pat-ti*
pa-ru-ka ez-zu šam-ru ZÁLAG-*ka at-ta-ma ta-nam-din-ši-na-*[*ti*]
tuš-te-šìr te-re-te-ši-na ina ni-⸢*qí*⸣*-i áš-ba-ta*
a-na IM LÍMMU.BA *ar-kàt-si-na ta-par-ra-as*
kal se-he-ep da-ád-me ⸢*uz*⸣*-ni-ši-na tuš-pat-ti*
ma-la kap-pa ni-ṭi-il IGI.2-*ka ul im-ṣu-ú šá-ma-mu*
ma-la ma-kal-ti ba-ru-ú-ti ul im-ṣa-a gi-mir-ši-na KUR.MEŠ
ina UD-20-KÁM *re-šá-ta il-la-ta ù hi-da-a-ti*
tak-kal ta-šat-ti el-la ku-ru-un-ši-na ši-kar se-bi-ʾi-i ka-a-ri
i-naq-qa-nik-ka ši-kar sa-bi-ʾi ta-mah-har
šá la-mu-ši-na-a-ti dan-nu a-gu-ú tu-še-zib at-ta
el-lu-ú-tu$_4$ eb-bu-ú-ti sír-qé-ši-na tam-tah-har
ta-šat-ti mi-zi-iʾ-ši-na ku-ru-un-n[*a*]
ṣu-um-mi-rat ik-pu-du tu-šak-šad at-ta
šu-ut ik-kam-sa el-let-si-na ta-paṭ-ṭar

šu-ut ik-tar-ra-ba	*ik-ri-bi-ši-na tam-ta-har*
ši-na-ma pal-ha-ka	⌜*iš*⌝*-tam-ma-ra zi-kir-k*[*a*]
tar-ba-ti-ka i-dal-lal	*a-na da-riš*
sak-la-a-ti šá li-šá-na	*da-bi-bu ṣa-l*[*íp-tí*]
šá GIM DUNGU.MEŠ	*la i-ša-a pa-na u b*[*a-b*]*a*
šu-ut i-ba-ʾu	*er-ṣe-ti* DAGAL-*tì*
šu-ut ú-kab-bi-su	KUR.MEŠ *e-lu-ú-ti*
^{d}*làh-mu šu-ut* A.AB.BA	*šá ma-lu-ú pu-luh-ta*
e-ri-ib A.⌜AB.BA⌝	*šá* ABZU *i-ba-ʾu-ú*
mi-hir-ti ÍD *šá ir-te-du-ú*	^{d}UTU *ina mah-ri-ka*
a-a-ú-tu hur-sa-a-nu	*šá la lit-bu-šu šá-ru-ru-ka*
a-a-ta kib-ra-a-tu$_4$	*šá la iš-tah-ha-nu na-mir-ta* UD.DA-*ka*
muš-par-du-ú e-ṭu-tu$_4$	*muš-na-mir uk-li*
pe-tu-ú ek-le-ti	*muš-na-mir* KI-*tì* DAGAL-*tì*
mu-šah-lu-ú u$_4$*-mu mu-še-rid an-qul-lu*	*ana* KI-*tì qab-lu u*$_4$*-me*
mu-šah-miṭ ki-ma nab-li	KI-*tì ra-pa-áš-tu*$_4$
[*m*]*u-kar-ru-ú u*$_4$*-me*	*mu-ur-ri-ku* GE$_6$.MEŠ
mu-šal-biš ku-ṣu hal-pa-a	*šu-ri-pa šal-gi*
pe-tu-ú KÁ.GAL *sik-kur* AN-*e*	*muš-pal-ku-u da-lat da-ád-me*
mu-še-lu-u up-pi sik-ka-ta	*nam-za-qí áš-kut-ta*
mu-šak-ṣib la ba-bil pa-ni	*šá-ri-ku ba-la-ṭi*
[*x x x*] *šal-la ina te-še-e*	*qa-bal mu-ú-t*[*i*]
[*x x x x ṭ*]*è-me mit-lu-ku*	*ši-tul-ta mil-k*[*u*]
[*x x x x d*]*i-pa-ri še-re-e-ti*	*a-na* UN.MEŠ *n*[*é-bi-ma*]
[*x x x x*] *x* ⌜*iš-da*?⌝*-at* GIŠ.NÍG.GIDRU	*ku-us-si-i pa-le-e* LU[GAL-*ú-ti*]
[*mam-ma*]-⌜*an*⌝ ^{d}*í-gì*!*-gì*!	*ul šá-ni-in e-mu-q*[*a-ka* (*x x*)]
⌜^{d}*a-num* ^{d}*en-líl u* ^{d}*é-a*⌝	*li-šar-*[*bu-ú*] MU-*ka*
[*x x lì*]*b*?*-ba-k*[*a ha*]*-an-šá-a*	*a-*[*x x x x x*] *x-ka*

[^{d}*be*]-⸢*let*⸣-DINGIR.MEŠ *ba-ni-tu*$_4$ DINGIR.M[EŠ] *li-*[*šá-tir b*]*e-*⸢*lut*⸣*-ka*

[*ana* É.BABB]AR.RA *nam-ri* *šu-bat* *ta-ši-la-ti-ka*

[*x x*] *x x x x* *nap-tan* *kib-ra-a-ti*

[LUGAL *ša*]*k-ka-*⸢*nak*⸣*-ku* *e-nu* *u* *ru-bu-u*

[*x x a-n*]*a mah-r*[*i-k*]*a* *bi-lat-su-nu* *liš-šu-ka*

[*x x*] É.BABBAR.RA *ina ni-qé-e* *hi-ṣib* *ma-ta-a-ti*

[*x x*] *x ina* ⸢KUR$^{?}$⸣ *pa-rak-ka-ka* *li-te-di-iš*

[*x*] *x x ka an* ⸢*num*$^{?}$⸣ *šá la in-nen-nu-u* *qí-bit pi-šú*

[^{d}*a*]*-a kal-la-ti* GAL-*ti* *ina* É KI.NÁ *maš-ta-ki-*⸢*šá*⸣ *nu-uh liq-bi-ka*

TRANSCRIPTION

1 *mušnammir gimir šamāmī*
2 *mušaḫli ekleti ana nišī eliš u šapliš*
3 *Šamaš mušnammir gimir šamāmī*
4 *mušaḫli ekleti ana nišī eliš u šapliš*
5 *saḫpū kīma šuškalli erṣeta šarūrūka*
6 *ša ḫuršānī bērūti eṭ[ût]īšunu tušpardi*
7 *ana tāmartīka iḫdû ilū u malkū*
8 *iriššūka gimiršunu Igīgū*
9 *puzra sattakku šūḫuzū barīrūka*
10 *ina namirti ṣītīka kibissina inn[ammar]*
11 *melammūka ištene''û [šamāmī]*
12 *kibrāt erbetti kīma Girr[a ištaḫnā]*
13 *tušpalki bābī ša kalîš [parakkī]*
14 *ša kullat Igīgī nindabêšun[u tuštāšir]*
15 *Šamaš ana aṣîka kitmusā tenēšētu*
16 *uštep[per]ā ana nūrī[ka] gimiršina mātā[tu]*
17 *mušnammir pētû ekleti ṣerret šam[āmī]*
18 *mušaḫmiṭ zīq šāt urri mēreš ê napiš[ti] māti*
19 *šadî bērūti īrima šalummatka*
20 *namrirrūka imlû siḫip mātāti*
21 *šurrāta ana ḫursānī erṣeta tabarri*
22 *kippat mātāti ina qereb šamê šaqlāta*
23 *nišī mātāti kullassina tapaqqid*
24 *ša Ea šar malkī uštabnû kalîš paqdāka*
25 *šūt napišti šaknā mitḫāriš tere''i*
26 *attā-ma nāqissina ša eliš u šapliš*
27 *tētenettiq ginâ šamāmī*
28 *[š]umdulta erṣeta tabâ' ūmišam*
29 *mīl tâmti ḫursānī erṣeta šamāmī*
30 *kī takkassi ginâ tabâ' ūmišam*
31 *šaplâti malkī Kūbū Anunnakī tapaqqid*
32 *elâti ša [d]admē kalîšina tuštēšir*
33 *rē'û šaplâti nāqidu elâti*
34 *muštēšir nūr kiššati Šamaš attā-ma*
35 *tētenebbir tâmāta rapšata šadilta*
36 *[ša] Igīgī lā īdû qereb libbīša*
37 *[Šam]aš birbirrūka ina apsî ūridū*
38 *[laḫm]ū šūt tâmti inaṭṭalū nūrka*

39 *šadî [k]īma qê kasâta kīma imbari [ka]tmāta*
40 *rapšu andullaka saḫip [mā]tāti*
41 *tātašuš ūmišam-ma ul i'addarū pānūka*
42 *tuštabarri ina mūšim-ma tušaḫmiṭ [ukl]a*
43 *[a]na šiddī ša lā idî nesûti u bērī lā man[ûti]*
44 *Šamaš dalpāta ša urra tallika u mūša tassaḫra*
45 *[u]l ibašši ina gimir Igīgī ša šūnuḫu balīka*
46 *[in]a ilī napḫar kiššati ša šūturu kīma kâta*
47 *[ṣ]ītukka ipḫurū ilī māti*
48 *[n]amurratka ezzetu māta saḫpat*
49 *[š]a? napḫar mātāti šūt šunnâ lišāna*
50 *[tī]de kipdīšina kibissina naṭlāta*
51 *[kams]ānikka kullassina tenēšētu*
52 *[Ša]maš ana nūrīka ṣummurat mitḫartu*
53 *[ana] mākalti bārûti ana rikis erēni*
54 *[ana] mušemmî šā'ili pāšir šunāti*
55 *[...]... ša riksāti kitmusū maḫarka*
56 *[ina maḫ]rīka kitmusū raggu u kīnu*
57 *[mannu?] urradu ina apsî balīka*
58 *[ša e]bbi kīni u zāmânê tušāpi dīnšu[n]*
59 *arikta napišti ragg[i t]usāq u tuš[akri]*
60 *ireḫḫīšum-ma šitta kīma ṣālili inappu[š kīnu]*
61 *tutarra ṣalpa ša lamû [ebiršu]*
62 *tušelli ina ḫubur ša dīni tiṣbutū [tuzakka dīnšun]*
63 *ina dīn kināti Šamaš ša taqbû[šināti]*
64 *šūpû zikrūka ul innennû pāna ul t[ubbal]*
65 *temmid ana allāki ša šupšuqat ur[uḫšu]*
66 *ana ēbir tâmti ādir agê tanaddi[n libba]*
67 *ḫarrānāti ša lā amrā ṣā'ida taš[appar]*
68 *[s]ulî terteneddi māḫira ša [šam]ši*
69 *tamkāra nāš kīsi ina edê tušēzib*
70 *tušelli ārid anzanunzê tušaškan kappa*
71 *munnabta munnarba māḫāzī tukallam*
72 *ḫarrānāti ša lā īdû tukallam šalla*
73 *ša ina puzrāt ṣēri attā tapaṭṭar*
74 *abka ša ina bīt ṣib[itti] nadû tukallamšu nūra*
75 *ša ilšu ittīšu [zenû t]usallam*
76 *ina amār têr[ēt]i uznāšina tušpatti*
77 *tēmid ana mar[ṣi] ša issuḫu adanšu*
78 *taparras ar[kāt]i taše''e napšāti*
79 *tubbal [...] ana nišīšu*
80 *ina kurnugê erṣeti [lā tār]i tuballaṭ mīta*
81 *ištarāti [š]absāti ana nišī [t]usallam*
82 *ṣīrātā-ma ul innennâ qibīt pîka*
83 *Šamaš ina šuškallīka ḫābila tasaḫḫap*
84 *ina gišparrīka lāpit dāmi ul uṣṣi*
85 *ša ana māmītīka lā ipallaḫu ...[... ...]*

ana lā ādir zākir šumīka dābib ṣalpā[ti]
tarṣat šētka rappu ina erṣeti kamārū-[ma?]
ša ana alti tappêšu iššû nīš ī[nīšu?]
ina ūm lā šīmāti ukarri mū[tu]
kunnaššu kippu zēru ukabba[s]
išširšu kakkakā-ma mušēziba ul ī[ši]
ina dinīšu ul izzazza abū[šu]
ina pî dayāni ul ippalū šunu aḫḫūšu
ina ḫuḫāri ša erî saḫip ul īde
ša kāṣir anzilli qarnāšu tuballa
ēpiš šiddi kāpida eni qaqqaršu
dayāna ṣalpa mēsera tukallam
māḫir ṭāti lā muštēšira tušazbal arna
lā māḫir ṭāti ṣābit abbūt enši
ṭāb eli Šamaš balāṭa uttar
dayānu muštālu ša dīn mīšari idīnu
ugammar ēkalla šubat rubê mūšabšu
nādin kaspi ana ṣibti ḫābilu mīnâ uttar
uštakaṣṣab ana nēmelim-ma uḫallaq kīsa
nādin kaspi ana šiddī rūqūti mutēr ištēn šiqli ana šelal[ti]
ṭāb eli Šamaš balāṭa ut[tar]
ṣābit zibānīti ēpiš ṣilipti
muštēnû aban kīsi ušaqqa ušappal
uštakaṣṣab ana nēmelim-ma uḫall[aq kīsa]
ša kīni ṣābit zibānīti mādā [...]
mimma šumšu mād qīšaššu [...]
ṣābit sūti ēpiš ṣil[ipti]
nādin šīqāti ana birīyi mušaddin atri
ina lā ūmīšu [a]rrat nišī ikaššassu
ina lā adannīšu i[š]šâl irašši bilta
makkūršu ul ibêl apilšu
ana bītīšu ul irrubū šunu aḫḫūšu
ummânu kīnu nādin ê ina [kabr]i? pāni ušattar dumq[a]
ṭāb eli Šamaš balāṭ[a] uttar
urappaš kimta mešrâ irašš[i]
kīma mê nagbi dārî zēr[šu] dā[ri]
ana ēpiš usāt dumqi lā mūdû [ṣa]lip[ti]
muštennû šaplâti ina masdari šak[in ina maḫrīka]
šūt lumni īpušū zēršunu u[l dāri?]
šūt ulla pīšunu šakin ina maḫrīka
tušaḫmaṭ ṣīt pîšunu tapaššar attā
[t]ašemme tebêršināti ša ruggugi tumassa dīnšu
manāma mamma puqqudū qātukka
tuštešššer têrētīšina ša šukṣuru tapaṭṭar
tašemme Šamaš suppâ sullâ u karāba
šukenna kitmusa litḫuša u labān appi
ana ḫurri pîšu dunnamû išassīka

133 *ulālu enšu ḫubbulu muškēnu*
134 *ummisalla masdara ginâ imaḫḫarka*
135 *ša rūqat kimtašu nesû ālûšu*
136 *ina šurubat ṣēri rē'û imaḫḫarka*
137 *kaparru ina tēšî nāqidu ina nakri*
138 *Šamaš imaḫḫarka alaktu ētiqu puluḫti*
139 *tamkāru allāku samallû nāš kīsi*
140 *Šamaš imaḫḫarka bā'iru katimti*
141 *ṣayādu māḫiṣu muterru būli*
142 *ina būnzerri usandû imaḫḫarka*
143 *muttaḫlilu šarrāqu muṣallû ša šamši*
144 *ina sulê ṣēri muttaggišu imaḫḫarka*
145 *mītu murtappidu eṭemmu ḫalqu*
146 *Šamaš imḫurūka talteme kalāma*
147 *ul takli šūt imḫurūka taqīš taddin*
148 *ana yâti Šamaš lā tazêršināti*
149 *ša ad*[*n*]*āti Šamaš uznīšina tušpatti*
150 *pārūka ezza šamra nūrka attā-ma tanaddinšinā*[*ti*]
151 *tuštēšer têrētīšina ina nīqî ašbāta*
152 *ana šār erbetti arkassina taparras*
153 *kal seḫep dadmē uznīšina tušpatti*
154 *mala kappi niṭil īnīka ul imṣû šamāmū*
155 *mala mākalti bārûti ul imṣâ gimiršina mātātu*
156 *ina ešrê rīšāta illata u ḫidâti*
157 *takkal tašatti ella kurunšina šikar sēbî kāri*
158 *inaqqânikka šikar sābî tamaḫḫar*
159 *ša lamûšināti dannu agû tušēzib attā*[1]
160 *ellūti ebbūti serqīšina tamtaḫḫar*
161 *tašatti mizi'šina kurunn*[*a*]
162 *ṣummirāt ikpudū tušakšad attā*
163 *šūt ikkamsā ellessina tapaṭṭar*
164 *šūt iktarrabā ikribīšina tamtaḫḫar*
165 *šinā-ma palḫāka ištammarā zikirk*[*a*]
166 *tarbâtīka idallalā šina ana dāriš*
167 *saklātu ša lišāna dābibū ṣal*[*ipti*]
168 *ša kīma erpēti lā īšâ pāna u b*[*āb*]*a*
169 *šūt ibā'ū erṣeta rapašta*
170 *šūt ukabbisū šadî elûti*
171 *laḫmū šūt tâmti ša malû puluḫta*
172 *erib tâmti ša apsâ ibā'ū*
173 *meḫerti nāri ša irteddû Šamaš ina maḫrīka*
174 *ayūtu ḫursānū ša lā litbušū šarūrūka*
175 *ayātu kibrātu ša lā ištaḫḫanā namirta ṣētka*
176 *mušpardû eṭûti mušnammir ukli*
177 *pētû ekleti mušnammir erṣeti rapašti*

---

[1] Ms. BabLBSch10 has a variant: *ša tarammūšināti ina danni ag*[*ê tušēzib attā*].

178 *mušaḫlû ūmi mušērid anqulli ana erṣeti qablu ūmi*
179 *mušaḫmiṭ kīma nabli erṣeti rapašti*
180 *[m]ukarrû ūmī murrik mušâti*
181 *mušalbiš kūṣa ḫalpâ šurīpa šalga*
182 *petû abulli sikkūr šamê mušpalkû dalāt dadmī*
183 *mušēlû uppi sikkati namzāqi aškutti*
184 *mušakṣib lā bābil pāni šārik balāṭi*
185 [...] *šalla ina tēšî qabal mūt[i]*
186 [... *ṭ]ēmi mitluki šitūlti milk[i]*
187 [... *d]ipār šērēti ana nišī n[ebī-ma]*
188 [...]... *išdāt*$^{?}$ *ḫaṭṭi kussî palê ša[rrūti]*
189 *[mamm]an*$^{?}$ *Igīgī ul šānin emūq[āka* (...)]
190 *Anu Enlil u Ea lišar[bû] zikirka*
191 [... *li]bbak[a*$^{?}$ *ḫ]anšā* ... [... ...]...*ka*
192 *[Bē]let-ilī bānīt ilī li[šātir b]ēlūtka*
193 *[ana Ēbabb]ari namri šubat tašīlātīka*
194 [...] ... *naptan kibrāti*
195 *[šarru ša]kkanakku enu u rubû*
196 [... *an]a maḫr[īk]a bilassunu liššûka*
197 [...] ... *Ēbabbara ina niqê ḫiṣib mātāti*
198 [...]... *ina māti*$^{!?}$ *parakkaka līteddiš*
199 [...]... ... *ša lā innennû qibīt pîšu*
200 *[u A]ya kallātu rabītu ina bīt mayāli maštakīša nūḫ liqbīka*

TRANSLATION[2]

1 Illuminator of the whole of heaven,
2 Who makes light the darkness for the peoples, above and below,
3 Šamaš, illuminator of the whole of heaven,
4 Who makes light the darkness for the peoples, above and below,
5 Your radiance spreads out like a net over the world,
6 You brighten the gloom of the distant mountains.
7 Gods and netherworld gods are glad at your appearance,
8 All the Igigi-gods rejoice in you.
9 Your beams unerringly provide the clue to secret places,
10 At the brightness of your rising people's footprints are rev[ealed].
11 Your dazzle seeks out [the heavens],
12 The four world regions [are warmed up], as if with fire.
13 You open up the gates of every [sanctuary],
14 You [regulate] the food offerings of all the Igigi-gods.
15 O Šamaš, humankind kneels to your rising,
16 All lands best[ir] themselves towards [your] light.
17 Illuminator of darkness, opener of the bosom of hea[ven],
18 Who lets the breeze of morn bring lustre to the grainfields, life of the land,
19 Your splendor envelops the distant mountains,
20 Your brilliance fills all the lands.
21 Leaning over the mountains, you inspect the earth,
22 In heaven, you hold the disk of the world in balance.
23 You make the people of all lands your charge,
24 Those that Ea, sovereign of kings, has created are wholly entrusted to you.
25 You shepherd all living creatures together,
26 You are their herdsman, those above and below.
27 You cross regularly through the heavens,
28 Every day you traverse the vast earth.
29 High seas, mountains, earth, and sky,
30 You traverse them regularly, every day, as if they were pavement.
31 In the lower regions you take charge of the netherworld gods, the demons, the Anunna-gods,
32 In the upper regions you administer all the inhabited world.
33 Shepherd of the lower regions, herdsman of the upper regions,

[2] By B. R. Foster; this is an updated version to his earlier *Before the Muses*, [3]2005 edition, 627-635.

34 You, Šamaš, administer the light for all.
35 You cross regularly the wide expanse of the seas,
36 [Whose] depths not even the Igigi-gods know.
37 [O Šam]aš, your radiance goes down to the deep,
38 [The monste]rs of the ocean can see your light.
39 You bind mountains together like a cord, you [bl]anket (them) like a haze,
40 Your broad protection is cast over the [la]nds.
41 Though your face fall each day, never is it wholly eclipsed,
42 At night you are still there, you light up [the darkness].
43 [T]o far-off regions unknown and for count[less] leagues
44 You persevere, O Šamaš, what you went by day you come back at night.
45 Among all the Igigi-gods there is [no]ne who does such wearisome toil but you,
46 Nor [amo]ng the gods of the entire universe is one who does so much as you!
47 At your rising the gods of the land assemble,
48 While your fierce glare covers the land.
49 Of all the lands of different tongues,
50 [You] know their intentions, you can see their footprints.
51 All humankind [kneels] before you,
52 [O Ša]maš, everyone longs for your light,
53 [At] the diviner's bowl, at the knotted sprigs of cedar,
54 [At] the roasting pot (of offerings set out) by the dream interpreter, who explains visions of the night,
55 [*Those who are preparing for*] rites kneel before you.
56 [Bef]ore you kneel both wicked and just.
57 [Who] goes down to the depths but you?
58 You clear up the case [of] the innocent truth-teller and (his) opponent,
59 You give [short] shrift to the wicked,
60 Slumber creeps over the [just], he breathes like a man in repose.
61 You turn back the rogue who is a hindrance [to his friend],
62 You rescue from the brink of hell the one tied up in a lawsuit, [you clear their case].
63 Whatever you say [to them (scil. humankind)] in just verdict, O Šamaš.
64 Your utterances are manifest, they cannot be changed, you [show] no favoritism.
65 You give support to the traveler who[se] jour[ney] is trying,
66 To the seafarer in dread of the waves you grant [courage],
67 You *s*[*end off*] the roamer on unexplored routes,
68 You keep guiding on the trail any who turn toward the [Su]n.
69 You rescue from the flashflood the merchant bearing (his) purse,
70 You bring up the one gone down to the deep, you set wings (upon him).
71 You show havens to refugees and runaways,
72 You show the prisoner roads he did not know,
73 You deliver the one (lost) in wilderness recesses,
74 To the captive cast in pris[on] you show the light.

75 [You] reconcile the one whose god [is angry] with him,
76 When they see a portent, you make people heed it well.
77 You attend the sick man whose normal term of illness has elapsed,
78 You diagnose the cause, you are watchful for (his) welfare,
79 You bear [*glad tidings of him*] to his family,
80 You bring the dying back to life, from the Land of No Return.
81 You reconcile angry goddesses with the people,
82 You are exalted, your command cannot be changed.
83 O Šamaš, you enmesh the evil-doer with your net,
84 From your toils no shedder of blood can escape.
85 He who, taking an oath by you, is not afraid to [...],
86 For the one who does not revere the invocation of your name, testified in false words,
87 Your net is spread, a snare in the earth, a *hunting trap* [*indeed*!]
88 The man who co[vets] his neighbor's wife,
89 Dea[th] cuts short his lifespan before his destined time,
90 A springe is set for him, that vicious man will step into it,
91 Your weapon makes straight for him, he will ha[ve] none to save him.
92 [His] father will not attend his trial,
93 Nor will his own brothers reply to the judge's queries,
94 He is caught unawares in a brazen trap!
95 You blunt the horns of the contriver of offenses,
96 The swindler plotting to work a draw, his foothold's undercut.
97 You show the roguish judge (the inside of) a jail,
98 He who takes the fee but does not carry through, you make him bear the punishment.
99 The one who receives no fee but takes up the cause of the weak,
100 Šamaš is pleased with him, he will prolong (his) life.
101 The scrupulous judge who gives just verdicts,
102 He will have a palace at his disposal, princely will be his dwelling.
103 What return will there be for the exploitive lender of money?
104 He will cause a decrease in profit and he will lose the principal.
105 He who invests long-term, who returns one shekel for thr[ee],
106 Šamaš is pleased with him, he will pro[long] (his) life.
107 He who cheats as he holds the scales,
108 Who switches weights, making them more or less,
109 He will cause a decrease in profit and he will lose the [principal].
110 The one who holds the balance honestly, many *are* [*his* ...],
111 However much (he weighs) will be given to him [*sevenfold*].
112 He who commits fra[ud] as he holds the dry measure,
113 Who makes loans by the medium standard, demands repayment by the extra standard,

114 Before his time, the people's curse shall take effect on him,
115 Before his date due, he shall be called to account, he shall bear the penalty:
116 His first-born son shall not take over his property,
117 His own brothers shall not succeed to his estate.
118 The honest creditor who makes loans by the [large] standard, he does extra good.
119 Šamaš is pleased with him, he will prolong (his) life,
120 He shall make (his) family numerous, he shall build up wealth,
121 [His] seed shall be perpe[tual] as the waters of a perpetual spring.
122 For the one who does good deeds, who knows no [de]cepti[on],
123 For the one who always uses different words from what he really means, it res[ts with you!]
124 The seed of evildoers shall n[ot abide].
125 The nay-sayers' testimonies are before you,
126 You quickly analyze what they have to say,
127 You hear and examine them, you detect the case of the villainous.
128 Each and every one is entrusted to your hands,
129 You set straight their omens, you resolve what perplexes.
130 You heed, O Šamaš, prayer, supplication, and blessing,
131 Obeisance, kneeling, whispered prayer, devotion.
132 The feeble one calls you as much as his speech allows him,
133 The meek, the weak, the oppressed, the wretched,
134 Daily, always, and steadily appeal to you.
135 (So too) the one whose family is remote from him, whose townsmen are far away.
136 The shepherd in dread of the wilderness appeals to you,
137 The herdsman in trouble, the keeper of sheep among the enemy.
138 O Šamaš, there appeals to you the caravan passing through danger,
139 The travelling merchant, the agent carrying (his) purse.
140 O Šamaš, there appeals to you the fisherman with (his) net,
141 The hunter, the beater, the one who drives the game,
142 The fowler among (his) snares appeals to you,
143 The footpad, the robber are prayerful to the Sun,
144 The bandit on the wilderness tracks appeals to you,
145 The wandering dead, the vagrant spirit appeal to you,
146 O Šamaš, you have listened to them all,
147 You did not reject those who appealed to you, you gave (them) largess.
148 For my sake, O Šamaš, do not despise these people!
149 You have opened wisdom, O Šamaš, to the world,
150 You yourself grant people who seek you your fierce and burning light.
151 You set straight their omens, you preside over sacrifices.
152 You probe their future to the four cardinal points,
153 You have opened wisdom to the entire inhabited world.
154 The heavens are too puny to be the cup of your gazing,

155 All the lands are too puny to be (your) seer's bowl.
156 On the twentieth of the month you rejoice with mirth and joy,
157 You dine, you drink their fine brew, the brewer's beer at wharf side,
158 They pour out barkeep's beer for you, you accept it.
159 You are the one who saved them, surrounded by mighty waves,
160 You accept from them in return their fine, clear libations.
161 You drink their sweet beer and beverage,
162 You are the one who lets them realize their hopes.
163 You pardon the kin of those who kneel to you,
164 You accept the prayers from those who regularly say their prayers (to you).
165 It is they who revere you, they extol your name,
166 They praise your greatness forever.
167 Those of barbarous tongue, who speak bewildering words,
168 Those people who, like clouds, are faceless and unapproachable,
169 Those men who traverse the wide earth,
170 Those who have tramped the high[3] mountains,
171 Monsters from the sea, filled with fearsomeness,
172 Denizens of the ocean, who traverse the depths,
173 The catch of the rivers, they are what they lead, O Šamaš, before you.
174 Which are the mountains that are not arrayed in your beams?
175 Which are the corners of the earth that are not warmed by the brightness of your rising?
176 Brightener of gloom, illuminator of shadow,
177 Penetrator of darkness, illuminator of the wide world,
178 Who makes daylight radiant, who sends down the heat glare of midday to the earth,
179 Who makes the wide world glow like flame,
180 Who can shorten the days and lengthen the nights,
181 Who blankets (the earth) with cold, frost, ice, (and) snow,
182 Who opens the gate (and) the bolt of heaven, opens wide the doors of the inhabited world,
183 Who lifts the socket and the pin, the latchkey, and the bolt,
184 Who shrivels the relentless, who bestows life,
185 [Who ...] the captive in combat, a fight to the death.
186 [Who ... re]ason, counsel, deliberation, advice,
187 [Who lights the t]orch of daybreak, gl[owing] for the people.
188 [Who upholds] ... scepter, throne, rule, (and) dy[nasty],
189 No[ne] among the Igigi-gods can rival [your] strength.
190 May Anu, Enlil, and Ea glori[fy] your name,
191 [(...)] your *he*[*art*], the fifty *A*[*nunna-gods* ...] you,
192 May [Be]let-ili, who created the gods, [extend] your dominion.
193 [In] radiant [Ebabb]ar, your splendid abode,

[3] Variant: "inviolable".

194 […] … a banquet *from* the four world regions.
195 [May king, go]vernor, high priest, and prince,
196 […] before you, may they bring you their tribute.
197 […] Ebabbar, in offerings, the yield of the lands,
198 […] in the *land*, may your throne dais be ever renewed,
199 […] … whose utterance cannot be changed,
200 May [A]ya, the great bride, say to you in the bed chamber of her living quarters, "Rest!"

COMMENTARY

This philological commentary is an expanded version, with some modifications, of the "Notes" section from the online edition of the Šamaš Hymn. The digital "Notes" are still available on the eBL platform (Rozzi 2021a: https://www.ebl.lmu.de/corpus/L/3/4/SB/-). The current commentary includes linguistic notes on the text, interpretations of certain problematic verses, and references to secondary bibliography.

17. The line presents an inverted word order and should probably be read as *mušnammir ekleti pētû ṣerret šam*[*āmī*], see Borger 1964, 55. The same phrase *ṣerret ša-ma-mi*, "the udders of Heavens", is attested in a literary Hymn to Marduk (Marduk 2), ll. 9-10, see Lambert 1960b, 61. Cf. also Lambert 1960a, 318-319 and Oshima 2011, 240-241. See Horowitz 1998, 253 for further attestations of this expression.

18. For the reading *zīq šāt urri*, see Seux 1976, 53, fn. 15, in which *zīq* is taken as *zīqu*, "breeze" (*AHw* 1532; *CAD* Z 133). Compare also Castellino 1977, 386, who reads SIK-*kur urri*, translating "Illustri, apri le tenebre, (sciogli) la corda (della serratura) del [cielo]". I follow the interpretation of Seux, since the motif of the deity providing a propitious breeze (often as a symbol of protection and divine benevolence) is well attested in hymns, cf. for example l. 175 of the Great Nabû Prayer: *ana kal māti ummāti ušaḫlâ manīt*[*u*], "You let a fair breeze gladden, for the whole land, the dogdays of summer" (Rozzi 2022a) and l. 87 of Marduk 2, *ašar anqullu isḫupu tušaḫla ūma*, "In the place shrouded in haze, you clear the day" (I am thankful to E. Jiménez for this line of Marduk 2). Considering these parallels, it is plausible that *mušaḫmiṭ* here should be derived from *ḫamāṭu* "to burn" (*CAD* Ḫ 64-65 sub *ḫamāṭu* B; *AHw* 316b sub *ḫamāṭu* III), rather than from *ḫamāṭu* "to hasten" (*CAD* Ḫ 62-63 sub *ḫamāṭu* A; *AHw* 316a sub *ḫamāṭu* II). Since a meaning such as "to burn" is not applicable in the present context, one could hypothesize a more figurative meaning, like "to make glow," as suggested in Jiménez 2017, 250 on l. 24: *marmāḫu ina libbiya upuntašu ušnammar ārir ana paššūr ilī u šarri ú-šaḫ-ma-ṭu ginâšu*, "using me, the m.-priest makes his flour offering splendid. The miller(?) makes glowing his regular offering for the table of the gods and the king" (cf. also eSAD by Streck et al., sub *ḫamāṭu* III).

21. *šurrāta* was formerly analyzed as *aʾāru* Št (Lambert 1960a, 319) or as *šurru* (Frankena 1962, 164, *AHw* 1285a). The latter verb, i.e. *šurru*, "to lean down", seems to suit better the present context. See Foster and George 2020, 49, base 9 for a new attestation of *šurru* in the feminine participle form *mu-ši-ra-at*, and compare also the recent entry in eSAD by Streck *et al.*, sub Š; Rowton (1962, 276b) suggested to read *kadrāta*, translating "dominant over the mountains you survey the earth", but this interpretation seems unlikely, as a reading KAD of ŠU is hardly attested. The image conveyed in this line is of the Sun God leaning down towards the earth, observing everything and everyone below him. This topos is commonly found in other Mesopotamian compositions dedicated to the Sun, such as the Kiutu prayers (Baragli 2022a, 107-108, with further references).

26. Ms. SipNB3a omits *ša*.

31. This line is quoted in a commentary on the medical series Sagig 4 (here SipLBQuo1), where an explanation of the name of ^{d}*kù-bu* is given, deriving it from the verb *naṣāru*, "to guard". Indeed SipLBQuo1, obv. 7 reads: [(*x*)] KÙ$^{?}$ (:) KI-*tì* : SU$^{?}$: *na-ṣa-ri : šap-la-a-tú ma-al-ku* ^{d}*kù-bi* ^{d}*a-nun-na-ki ta-paq-qid* : SAG.⸢KI⸣ [*x* (*x*)], "[(...)] KÙ (?) means "Netherworld" and SU (?) means 'to guard', (as in) 'In the depth you review the Anunnaki, the princes of Kūbu'", see the edition and translation of this tablet in Jiménez 2016, CCP 4.1.4.B. On the alleged connection between the word *Kūbu* and the verb *naṣāru*, see Jiménez and Schmidtchen 2017, 233. The quotation in SipLBQuo1 allows to restore a parallel passage occurring in another tablet (BM 40837+), also identified as a commentary on Sagig 4, and here named BabLBQuo1, obv. l. 2′: [...] *x*-⸢*si*⸣ : KÙ : KI-*tì* [: SU$^{?}$: *na-ṣa-ri* : *šap-la-a-tú ma-al-ku* ^{d}*kù-bu*$^{?}$ ^{d}*a-nun-na-ki ta-paq-qid* : SAG.⸢KI⸣ [*x* (*x x*)]. For the edition of this tablet, see Jiménez and Schmidtchen 2017. Cf. Frahm, Frazer and Jiménez 2016, CCP 4.1.4.C. Furthermore, line 31 of the present hymn is also quoted in a commentary on the menological series *Iqqur īpuš* (DT.35, here BabLBQuo2), in which it is used to explain the noun *malku* as the god Nergal or as the Anunnaki (BabLBQuo2, obv. l. 24): *šá-niš ma-al-ku* : ^{d}U.GUR : *šá šap-la-a-tú mál-ku* ⸢^{d}⸣⸢*kù*⸣-⸢*bu*⸣ ^{d}*a-nun-na-ki ta-paq-qid.* See Frahm, Frazer and Jiménez, 2013: CCP 3.8.2.B with further references, cf. Rozzi 2021a.

37. The image of the Sun God's light penetrating the depths of the sea finds a parallel in a verse of a Sumerian poem on the goddess Inanna and the king Išme-Dagan. One verse of the composition describes the goddess in her manifestation as Venus, obv. l. 8: a ab-ba-ke$_4$ šu ki-in-dar di an-bar$_7$-GANA$_2$ ḫe$_2$-ši-še$_3$-ĝal$_2$, "Parting the waters of the sea, turning the morning light into darkness(?)", see Ludwig and Metcalf 2017, 7, 9 and 14. I am thankful to C. Metcalf who pointed out this parallel to me.

41. For the interpretation of this line, see *CAD* A/1 107 sub *adāru* A, mng. 8b and *CAD* A/2 423 sub *ašāšu* A, mng. d, where the readings [*t*]*a-ta-šu-uš* and *pa-n*[*u-k*]*a* are suggested, cf. also Seux 1976, 55, 25 and 26, and Foster 2005, 629. The recently identified fragment K 19543 (NinNA3c) confirms the reading [*t*]*a-ta-šu-uš*, therefore the reconstruction proposed by Lambert in his edition of the text, namely [*l*]*a ta-šu-uš*, can now be dismissed (Lambert 1960a, 128). Furthermore, Lambert suggests the reading *pa-r*[*u*]*-ka* – from *pāru*, "skin" – at the end of the line (Lambert 1960a, 128, "nor is your *surface* darkened"). However, such an abstract meaning, i.e., "surface" or similar, is never attested for the noun *pāru* (see *CAD* P 209; cf. *AHw* 836), and the reading *pa-n*[*u-k*]*a* seems more likely.

42. Von Soden (1977, 281) proposed the reading *tu-šaḫ-bat* from the Š-stem of *ḫabātu* (*AHw* 304a III), suggesting that a preterite would be unlikely within the line because of the preceding present form *tuš-ta-bar-ri*. However, sequences of durative and preterite verbs are commonly found in literary passages where the preterite has a gnomic aspect (see Mayer 1992, 380 on the gnomic preterite in Akkadian). The form *tu-šaḫ-miṭ* in the present line, therefore, can be explained as a gnomic preterite. Additionally, the verb *ḫamāṭu* (*AHw* 316-317 under *ḫamāṭu* III; *CAD* Ḫ 64-65 under *ḫamāṭu* B) occurs two other times within the hymn (lines 18 and 179), further supporting *tu-šaḫ-miṭ* as the *lectio facilior*.

43. Ms. NinNA1: *ù ana* DANNA (KASKAL.GÍD).

54. For the interpretation of this line I follow Mayer 2017, 11. Mayer takes *mu-ši-mi* (NinNA2b, i l. 38′), and its variants [*mu-š*]*im-me* (NinNA1, i l. 54) and [*mu*]-*šim-ma* (BabLBSch8, rev. 1″), as an elsewhere unattested word derived from *šawûm*, "to roast" (*AHw* 1206 and 1590; *CAD* Š/I 350), namely *mušemmû*. Mayer translates this term as "roasting plate" ("Röstplatte") and suggests it parallels [*ana*] *mākalti bārûti* in the preceding line. Lines 53-54 would thus form a parallel couplet of the synthetic type (see § 4.1.7 in the introduction).

55. There are approximately three signs missing at the beginning of the line. Böhl (1942, 676) suggests restoring the participle *rākisu*, translating "wie den ritus vervullen." Compare the interpretation offered by Foster, who understands *rik-sa-a-ti* as related to legal bonds, translating: "[The parties to] contracts kneel before you" (Foster 2005, 630), and similarly Hecker, who offers: "Die Verträge [schließen], liegen vor dir auf den Knien" (Hecker 2013, 68). The lacuna prevents from a certain reconstruction of the line but considering the mention of the ritual experts in the verses immediately preceding, Böhl's interpretation seems probable.

57. For the restoration of this line, see Schollmeyer 1912, 81 and Böhl 1942, 676.

61. Since at least part of the text is likely to have been composed in the Old Babylonian period, the term *ibru* is perhaps best understood as "person of equal status," "peer," or "fellow," rather than in its more "emotional" sense typical of the first millennium, "friend." On this see CAD I 7.

62. Ms. BabLBSch5 reads ⸢*ḫu-bur*⸣ *šá* ⸢*ina*⸣.

71. On this line, see Lambert 2004, 214 (reconstruction by W.R. Mayer).

74. Ms. BabLBSch1 omits *ina*.

76. For the use of *amāru* with *têrtu* compare *CAD* A/2 14 s.v. *amāru* 2f 2′.

77. BabLBSch1 (BM 33465), obv. 13′ shows the variant form [*t*]*e-e*[*m-mi-id.*

78. For the interpretation of *taše"e napšāti*, cf. SB Gilgameš XI, 25: *muš-šìr mešrâm* (NÍG.TUKU)-*ma še-'-i napšāti* (ZI.MEŠ), "abandon riches and seek survival!", George 2003, 704-705. Cf. Rozzi 2021b, 222.

80. This line is preserved in an incomplete manner in all the manuscripts that contain it. However, the school fragment BabLBSch1 and the library manuscript from Nineveh NinNA1 preserve traces that allow for a hypothetical reconstruction of the text in the lacuna.

The fragment BabLBSch1 runs as follows (obv. 16′): [*ina*] KUR.⸢NU⸣.GI$_4$.⸢A⸣ *x* [*x x* (*x*)] *x tu-bal-l*[*a-ṭ*]*u* ⸢*mi*$^?$*-i-tu*$_4$⸣.

Although the sign following A is partially broken, three horizontal wedges and an oblique wedge are still visible. The traces could be reconciled with KI. Judging by the available space on the tablet, the lacuna could accommodate three or four additional signs. The sign preceding TU is also damaged, but faint traces of a final vertical wedge and a wedge-head suggest it could be the sign RI. One could reconstruct K[I$^?$-*tì la ta-r*]*i*$^?$ in the break,[4] based on a parallel in *Ištar's Descent*, l. 1: ⸢*a-na* KUR.NU⸣.GI$_4$.A *qaq-qa-ri l*[*a*$^?$ *ta-a-ri*$^?$] (Setälä 2022), cf. also the equation in the lexical sources, e.g. lú = *ša* II 65: KUR ⸢NU⸣-GI$_4$-A = *er-ṣe-et la ta-re-*[*e*] (MSL 12, 106, cf. *CAD* E 308 sub *erṣetum*, lex. section). Compare, furthermore, a first-millennium ritual for the divine ferryman of the netherworld (VAT 13656 + VAT 13657 // CMAwR 2, text 8.25, l. 224), rev. iv, 6: ⸢KUR⸣.NU.GI$_4$.A KI-*tì la ta-ri.*

The manuscript NinNA1 may confirm this reading, as it shows clear traces of KI after KUR.NU.GI$_4$.A (ii 13′): KUR.NU.GI$_4$.⸢A KI⸣-[*tì*$^?$ *x x x x x x x x* (*x*)].

---

[4] I owe this reading to Mikko Luukko, who also kindly pointed out to me the line in CMAwR 2, text 8.25, l. 224.

86. This line seems to show the textual variant *ṣīt pîka* in two manuscripts: BabNB1 obv. 11′: [*x x x x x ṣi*?*-it*?] ⸢*pi*⸣*-ka* and NinNA1 ii 19′: *ṣi*?*-i*]*t*? *pi*?*-ka*.

88. If the restoration at the end of the line is correct, the verse contains a *figura etymologica*. For a similar phrase, cf. l. 27 of *Šimâ milka*: *ē tešši īnīka ana aššat amēli*, "Don't covet another man's wife", see Cohen 2013, 86-87.

89. The meaning of this line is debated. Isolated, the form *ú-gar-ri/a* could also be read as *ú-šá-ri/a*, from *šurrû*, "to begin", as proposed by de Zorzi, 2022, 385-386, who translates the line as: "Before his appointed day he will begin [his?] (road to) dea[th]." However, consider the similar phrase found in an inscription of Ashurbanipal (Novotny and Jeffers 2018, Nr. 3, col. iv, l. 50; Nr. 4 col. iv, l. 19′; Nr. 6 col. 6, l. 75): *ina u*$_4$*-me la šim-ti-šú mu-u-tu ú-gar-ru-u*, var. *ú-ga-ru-u*.[5] The presence of this variant spelling suggests that the reading GAR is more likely. On the meaning of this formulation, see the interpretation of Novotny and Jeffers 2018, 67: "*mu-ú-tu ú-ga-ru-u* "whom death called": *CAD* G 62 sub *gerû* 2 provides a meaning of "to open up hostilities; to start a lawsuit" for this verb in the D stem (although it does not cite this passage). Thus, R. Borger (1996, 223) tentatively translates the phrase: "der den Tod vorzeitig ge...t (etwa: provoziert??) hatte." Note also that the verb *qerû* has a meaning "to invite; take away", which includes an OB euphemism for dying (*CAD* Q 242-243), although the verb is not presently attested in the D stem." Incidentally, the D-stem of *qerû* is now attested, see Mayer 1988, 162-163 ad 147, rev. l. 10′. Hence, a reading of the sign as *qàr* might also be possible. However, despite the well-attested euphemistic expression for the verb *qerû*, the value *qàr* for NÍG is attested infrequently, and only in the Neo-Assyrian period (see von Soden and Röllig 1991^{4}, 64). The most likely solution seems to be interpreting the form as *ukarri*, D-stem from *karû*, "to be(come) short," reading it as *ú*-KAR$_5$*-ri/a*. In fact, although the reading of KAR$_5$ for NÍG is quite rare, the alternation of the phonemes /q/ and /k/ is attested in both Middle and Neo-Assyrian sources (see, for example, the variation in the forms *ú-kar-ru-ú* and *ú-kar*$_5$*-ru-ú* in Middle Assyrian as shown by de Ridder 2017, 299, who suggests that the reading KAR$_5$ of NÍG in Middle Assyrian was probably derived from the value GAR, which rarely appears in MA texts and to which the value GÀR (QAR) is preferred. See also de Ridder 2018, 55. For Neo-Assyrian sources, see Luukko 2004, 71).

90. The spelling ŠE.NUMUN might initially suggest interpreting *zēru* as "seed." However, the reading *zēru* as "hated", deriving from *zêru*, "to despise", fits the context more appropriately. Furthermore, the manuscript NinNA2b – unlike the others that preserve this word, namely BabNB1 (obv. l. 15′ ŠE.NUM]UN), SipNB3b (ii l. 7′ ŠE.NU[MUN]) and SipNB4a (ii l. 10′ ŠE.NUMUN) – does not use a logogram

[5] I am thankful to N. Heeßel, who pointed out this parallel to me.

but instead spells the word as *ze-ru*. In this same manuscript, the logogram NUMUN appears in lines 121 and 124, where it clearly stands for "seed." This could imply that *ze-ru* in the current line should indeed be understood as *zēru* "hated." It is plausible that the Nineveh manuscript preserves the correct reading, while the Babylonian manuscripts employ an erroneous logographic spelling due to the homonymy of the two nouns. It cannot be ruled out, however, that the variant in the Babylonian manuscripts does not represent an error, but rather a case of deliberate, playful writing. Cf. Rozzi 2021a and 2022b, 153.

96. The collation of the new manuscripts (SipNB3b and SipNB4a) confirms that the line actually reads *e-piš šid-di*, thus the reading *ēpiš riddi* suggested by Frahm 2009, 42-44 and accepted by Mayer (see Mayer 2003, 239 and Mayer 2017, 222) must be dismissed. The manuscript BM 65472 (SipLB4a) reads ŠID-*du*, and not RID-*du* as defended by Mayer 2017, 222. The sense of the noun *šiddu* in the line under consideration is, however, obscure, since its main meaning "side", "edge" yields little sense in the present context. The interpretation of this word as *šeṭṭu*, "crime", allegedly a variant of the common noun *šettu*, as suggested in *CAD* Š/2 340, must be rejected, since *šeṭṭu* is a "ghost word," see Frahm 2009, 43.

99. The Assyrian manuscript from Nineveh (NinNA2b) reads *ṣa-bi-tú*, while the manuscripts from Sippar have *ṣa-bit* (SipNB3b and SipNB4a).

100. Worthington (2012, 187) proposes that the overhanging vowel in *ṭa-a-bi* (for *ṭāb*) which appears in most manuscripts, could represent a sandhi spelling reflecting the phonetic pronunciation of the word UGU (Akk. *eli)* immediately following. According to Worthington, the pronunciation of the first two words might have been */ṭābeli/*. Cf. also ll. 106 and 119 in MS NinNA1.

103. *mīnâ uttar*: This formula represents a topos in Akkadian wisdom literature, specifically in relation to the recurring motif of illicitly gained wealth. Similar thoughts can be found, for example, in *Šimâ milka*, ll. 33-36, cf. Cohen 2013, 86-87 and 105; compare, in particular, the similar phrases *mīna ilqe/talqe* "what will it gain?" (Cohen 2013, 86-87 l. 36; 88-89, l. 39; 98-99, l. 135′).

104. For the meaning "to diminish" of *šutakṣubu*, see Mayer 2017, 230.

105. For the reading *še-⸢la⸣-[ti]* see *AHw* 1335 and von Soden 1977, 281, but compare also Seux 1976, 58 fn. 58, where the reconstruction *še-n*[*a* is provided. Seux's reconstruction is followed by Reiner (1985, 75): "The moneylender who lends on long term and takes no more than two shekels for one" and Hecker (2013, 70): "Wer Silber auf langen Termin verleiht und einen Šeqel in (nur) zwei vermehrt". However, there is space for three signs at the end of the line, and the visible traces after ŠE before the break can be reconciled with LAL. Hence, the restoration *še*-⌜*lal*⌝-[*ti*] seems preferable.

108. Ms. SipNB4a adds *ù* between *ušaqqa* and *ušappal*.

112. For some remarks on the theme of divine retribution developed in ll. 112-117, see de Zorzi 2019, 172-178.

113. Ms. SipNB4a erroneously adds *la* after *a-na bi-ri-i*.

115. This line has been interpreted differently by scholars. Some attribute the moral nuance of "guilt" to the term *biltu*, generally translated as "load", "burden", "tribute" (*CAD* B 229-236; *AHw* 126). For instance, see Lambert's translation of the present line (1960a, 133; cf. also 321): "if he demanded repayment before the agreed date, there will be guilt upon him," cf. also Nurullin (2014, 218). Moran (1991, 330), on the other hand, takes *biltu* as *pištu*, "insult" (*CAD* P 433-434; *AHw* 869). However, considering the manuscript NinNA3b (ii, l. 8′), which preserves the logographic variant GU[N], the reading *biltu* seems more likely.[6]

As noted by de Zorzi (2019, 164-172), the figurative meaning of the term *biltu* is rarely attested, but in this context a more abstract interpretation seems plausible. Line 115 appears to mirror the one immediately preceding: a person who demands repayment in a dishonest way will receive only the "people's curse" (l. 114), and instead of payment, only a "burden", i.e., "a punishment", obtained before the due date.[7]

The use of the terms *adannu* and *biltu*, often found in commercial/economic documents, suits the context of the Hymn to Šamaš, where several expressions and terms related to commerce appear.[8]

Note, furthermore, that *irašši bilta* parallels *mešrâ irašši* in l. 120, which refers to what happens instead to the honest merchant: while the first acquires only a "punishment", consisting of a premature death and the loss of his goods, the second, on the other hand, obtains wealth.

---

[6] Moran (1991, 329) suggests taking the variant GU[N] as a scribal mistake, but considering the ambiguity of the context and the problematic nature of the interpretation, it is more prudent to rule out a scribal error.

[7] The phrase *ina lā ūmīšu* at line 114, literally meaning "before his time," could refer to an untimely death, as suggested by Nurullin (2014, 218), who furthermore understands *arrat nišī* as a metaphor for the universal destiny of mankind, i.e., death. The term *adannu* can have various meanings; it can indicate both the moment when a payment is expected to be made or received (*CAD* A/1 99-100, sub *adannu*; see also Lambert 1960a, 321) and the end of a human life (*CAD* A/1 98, sub *adannu* mng. 1, c). In this context, *ina lā adannīšu* parallels *ina lā ūmīšu*, and likely plays on the dual meaning of the creditor's expected payment date and the notion of dying before one's time.

[8] See Lambert 1960a, 321.

In addition, in her analysis of this passage of the Hymn to Šamaš, de Zorzi (2019, 175-176) considers the verbs *iššâl* and *iraššì* as a verbal pair. De Zorzi, following Lambert 1960a, 133, understands l. 115 as a conditional clause, translating ll. 115-117 as follows: "(If) he requests taking the yield (of the debtor's field) at a time not agreed upon / (then) his heir will not control his property, / his kin will not succeed to his estate".

However, other interpretations (e.g., Seux 1976, 58 and Foster 2005, 635), which take ll. 114-115 as a parallel couplet, seem preferable to me. These interpretations highlight the grammatical parallelism in the first hemistich of each line, where the phrase *ina lā ūmīšu* in l. 114 parallels *ina lā adannīšu* in l. 115. The two verses, because of their parallel structure, likely convey the same concept – namely, the punishment for trickery – and should therefore be read together as a cohesive unit. Note, moreover, that in the wisdom section of the text, those who perform just or unjust acts are always expressed either by a participle (e.g., l. 98 *māḫir ṭāti* and l. 99 *lā māḫir ṭāti*, l. 103 and l. 105 *nādin kaspi*, l. 108 *muštēnû*), a noun (e.g., l. 101 *dayānu muštālu*, l. 118 *ummânu kīnu*), or by the relative pronouns *ša* and *šūt* (e.g., l. 85, l. 88, l. 95, l. 124, l. 125). In other words, the subject is always explicitly stated. Considering the overall structure of the text, it seems therefore more likely that ll. 114-115 refer to the preceding couplet (ll. 112-113) and have as their subject "he who commits fra[ud] as he holds the dry measure" (*ṣābit sūti ēpiš ṣil*[*ipti*], l. 112), that is, the one "Who makes loans by the medium standard, demands repayment by the extra standard" (*nādin šīqāti ana birīyi (lā) mušaddin atri*, l. 113).

126. Note the hendiadys in *tušaḫmaṭ* …*tapaššar*. The manuscript SipNBSch3 (BM 55181), obv. l. 3′ reads *t*]*a-kaš-šad.*

128. Ms. NinNA3b adds *u* before *mamma.*

130-131. Ms. NinNA3b does not write the optional *u*.

134. I follow the reading *um-mi-sal-la*, as proposed in *CAD* U/W 120, *ummissalla* and Foster 2005, 632; see also Hecker 2013, 70 with fn. 67. Compare Lambert: *ummu šallu,* "she whose son is captive" (Lambert 1960a, 134-135). Ms. SipNB1 reads *ina mas-da-ri.*

135. Contrary to Lambert's interpretation, I understand URU-*ú-šú* as *ālû-šu*, "his fellow citizen" (*CAD* A/1 390), and not, as suggested by Lambert, as "his city" (see Lambert 1960a, 135: "He whose family is remote, whose city is distant"). I follow Deller, Mayer and Sommerfeld 1987, 206.

136. The word *šurubtu* has been interpreted as "eine Notlage" (von Soden 1977, 281, *AHw* 1287b) or as a variant of *šuribtu*, "terror" (see *CAD* Š/3 344). In addition, Hecker interprets it as a form derived from *erēbu*, "to enter", translating the line as follows: "der Hirte, [beim] Auftrieb in die Steppe wendet er sich an dich", see Hecker 2013, 70 with fn. 68. Considering *ina tešî* in the following line, and the occurrence of the word *puluḫtu* in l. 138, a meaning "fear", "terror", or similar, seems more likely. Cf. also Groneberg 1987, 72: "in der Kälte der Steppe", understanding *šurubtu* as connected with *šurīpu*/*šurbu*, "cold".

140. Here Mss. SipNB1 and AššNASch3 have *ina* before *katimti.*

143. For the translation of *šamši*, compare also the remarks by Dalley (1986, 99), who suggests taking this term as a title meaning "Your majesty", or "His majesty". I do not think it is necessary in the present context to translate the term *šamši* as a title, and I follow the most used translation for it, that is, "Sun", "Daylight" (see e.g., Foster 2005, 633; Hecker 2013, 71).

The meaning of *muṣallû* is debated, as some scholars (e.g. Lambert 1960a, 134; Reiner 1985; Foster 2005, 633; Hecker 2013, 71) consider it to be the rare term *muṣallû*, "liar", "evildoer", derived from *ṣelû* "to cheat" (*CAD* Ṣ 124; *AHw* 1090). In other cases, however, as in *CAD* S 367, it is derived from *s*/*ṣullû*, "to beseech", "to pray". Note, however, the blessing formula occurring in a Late Babylonian exercise tablet (YBC 11431, obv, 1-2a): $^{\text{lu2}}$IR$_3$^{meš}-*ka u*$_3$° *mu-ṣal-li-*⌜*i*⌝ *ša*$_2$ DINGIR^{me} "your servants and the ones praying to the gods" (Wagensonner 2020, 203). In light of the Late Babylonian exercise, it appears more likely that the term *muṣallû* is derived from *s/ṣullû*. However, the alternative hypothesis cannot be entirely dismissed. Moreover, the possibility of a double entendre cannot be ruled out, given that *muṣallû* in the sense of "liar" or "evildoer" would parallel *muttaḫlilu* and *šarrāqu* in the same line.

147. The Assur school manuscript AššNASch1 (VAT 10174), recently republished in Maul and Manasterska 2023, 112-120, no. 33, preserves the entire line (obv. 14) and allows the reconstruction of the disputed ending of the fragment: *ta-*⌜*qiš**⌝ *ta-din.* The two verbs form a hendiadys ("you gave (them) largess", literally "you gave and bestowed"). For occurrences of *qiāšu*(*m*) with *nadānu*, see *CAD* Q 157, sub 1. The reading suggested in Maul and Manasterska 2023, 113, i.e. *ta-*⌜*áp*⌝*-ta-tin*, in the sense of "you strengthened (them) time and again" ("du richtetest (sie) immer wieder auf"), can be dismissed, as the visible traces after TA can be reconciled with KIŠ (I owe this reading to T. Mitto). The syllabic reading *áp* (ÁB) is improbable, since it is rarely used in the 1st millennium (cf. von Soden and Röllig 1991, 245). Furthermore, the reading suggested here is confirmed by the Late Babylonian school tablet BabLBSch7 (BM 38061), obv. 6′ which reads: *ta-qi*]*š*$^{?}$ *ta-ad***-d*[*in**] (correcting Rozzi 2021b, 219).

150. For the interpretation of *pa-⸢ru$^{?}$⸣-ka* (SipNB1), *pár-ru-ka* (AššNASch1), as derived from *pârum*, "to seek", I follow *AHw* 836b, *CAD* P 210 sub *pâru* 1, Seux 1976, 61 and Maul and Manasterska 2023, 117. I take it as participle G-stem plural. Compare, however, also Mayer 2008, 98, who understands the form as derived from *parû*, "mule". The latter interpretation yields little sense in the present context.

152. Mss. SipNB1 and AššNASch1 read *a-na šá-a-ri er-bet-ti.*

153. SipNB1 (IM.124633), iii 24′ shows the variant *šá kal-la.*

154. AššNASch1 o 17′b has the variant *im-ṣu-šú*, probably a scribal error. For the possible pun in *kappi niṭil īnīka*, which would allude to *kappi īnī*, "eyelid", see Maul and Manasterska 2023, 118. Compare also the "Macranthropic" Hymn to Ninurta, l. 13: *kappi īnīka šarūr(ū) šamši ša šamê u erṣeta* [*saḫpu* (?)], "Your eyelids are the rays of the sun, which [cover] heaven and earth", Fadhil and Jiménez 2021, 198 and 203.

163. In the case of *el-let-si-na*, *CAD* K 120 suggests that the term may be a conflation of *ennetu* ("sin") (*CAD* E 169-170 and *AHw* 219; see also Mayer 2016, 205-206) and *illatu* ("group," "crew") (*CAD* I/J 82-85; *AHw* 372), providing the translation: "You pardon the sins of those who kneel down in supplication." This interpretation is also supported by Seux (1976, 61, fn. 61) and Oshima (2010, 154). However, some scholars interpret *el-let-si-na* exclusively as *illatu*, leading to the more literal translation "ranks". For example, see Westenholz (1997, 191) and Foster (2005, 634). Groneberg similarly understands *el-let-si-na* as *illatu*, but interprets the syntax differently, translating the line as "those who kneel down with their troops, you release" (Groneberg 1987, 61; Groneberg 1998, 18 and 19 fn. 8). Hecker offers a comparable translation: "Die (vor dir) niederknien, deren Gruppe löst du auf" (Hecker 2013, 71 with fn. 75). I propose an alternative interpretation, suggesting that *el-let-si-na* may be derived from *eʾiltu*/*iʾiltu* ("bond"), a term often associated with *paṭāru(m)*; cf. Lambert (2013, 322, and 324-325, l. 334): *lu-ú kul-lum a-na ilāni^{meš} ar-ku-ú-ti el-let-ki šá tap-ṭu-ru la tu-tar-ri* , "Let your bond, which you released and could not do up again, be shown to later gods".

Note that SipNBSch1 (BM 65461+) obv. 1′ features the variant ⸢*kam*^{v}⸣-⸢*sa*⸣.

166. Ms. BabLBSch13 adds *ši-na* before *ana dāriš*, but this seems a superfluous repetition in view of the previous line.

174. Ms. SipNB3a omits *ša* before *lā*.

187. Ms. NinNA1 omits *ana*.

188. The Sippar manuscript SipNB1 shows traces that could align with *iš-da-at* at the beginning of the line, although the poor condition of the tablet makes reading the signs difficult. An expression like *išdāt ḫaṭṭi* does not seem to be attested, but *išdu* frequently appears with the word *kussû*, "throne", which immediately follows *ḫaṭṭu* in the line under analysis (see *CAD* I 237, mng. 2 for attestations of *išdu* with *kussû*).

In the lacuna, a verb such as *kunnu*, "to make stable," might be expected, possibly in the participle form, given the series of participles that open lines 176-184. One could tentatively restore *mukīn* (suggestion by M. Luukko). For the use of *kunnu* with *išdu*, see *CAD* I 237, mng. 2′b. Note that the noun *palû* can yield not only the abstract meaning of "rule" or "period of office", as adopted in the translation used here, but also a more concrete meaning, probably the original, of "staff" or "rod". For the possible meanings of *palû*, see eSAD by Streck et al., sub *palû*. The latter meaning cannot be excluded in our text either.

190-192. For a parallel to these lines, cf. the incantation ritual published by Abusch and Schwemer 2011, 325 and 331, text no. 8.6.1., ll. 72′-73′ [...] ... *lišarbû zikirka* / [...] ... *ilī lišātir bēlūtka,* "may [...] praise your name / may [the ...] of the gods endow you with unrivalled lordship".

193. For the restoration of this line, see von Soden 1977, 281.

195. I follow George and Al-Rawi 1998, 202 for the restoration at the beginning of the line.

197. Ms. SipNB1 has no *ina*.

198. The phrase *parakkaka līteddiš* finds a parallel in Marduk 2, 45″ (Oshima 2011, 239, 252-253; collation E. Jiménez, personal communication).

GLOSSARY AND INDICES

Logograms and Their Readings

A.AB.BA → *tāmtu;* A.MEŠ → *mê;* ABZU → *apsû;*
dGIŠ.BAR → *Girru;* dUTU → *Šamaš;*
DAGAL → *rapšu;* DINGIR → *ilu;* DUNGU → *erpetu;*
EDIN → *ṣēru;* É → *bītu;* É.BABBAR.RA → *Ebabbar;* É.GAL → *ēkallu;*
GAL → *rabû;* GE_6 → *mūšu;* GEŠTU.2 → *uznu;* GIM → *kî, kīma;* GÍN → *šiqlu;* GIŠ.BÁN → *sūtu;* GIŠ.EREN → *erēnu;* GIŠ.NÍG.GIDRU → *haṭṭu;* GIŠ.TUKUL → *kakku;*
IBILA → *aplu;* ÍD → *nāru;* IGI.2 → *ēnu;* ILLU → *mīlu;* IM → *šāru;*
KÁ.GAL → *abullu;* KI → *erṣetu;* KI.NÁ → *maiālu;* KUR → *mātu;* KUR.NU.GI_4.A → *kurnugû;* KUŠ.NÍG.NA_4 → *kīsu;*
LÍMMU.BA → *erbettu;* LUGAL → *šarru;* LÚ.DAM.GÀR → *tamkāru;* LÚ.GIG → *marṣu;* LÚ.KÚR → *nakru;* LÚ.MUŠEN.DÙ → *ušandû;* LÚ.ŠÁMAN.LÁ → *šamallû;* LÚ.ŠU.HA → *bā'iru;*
MÁŠ.ANŠE → *būlu;* MÁŠ.GE_6 → *šuttu;* MU → *zikru;*
NA_4 → *abnu;* NIDBA → *nindabû;* NÍG.GA → *makkūru;* NUN → *rubû;* NUMUN → *zēru;*
PI → *pānu* B*;*
SUD → *rūqu;*
ŠEŠ → *ahu;*
TI.LA → *balāṭu;*
UD → *ūmu;* UD.DA → *ṣētu;* UGU → *eli;* UN.MEŠ → *nišē;* URU → *ālû;* UŠ → *redû;*
ZÁLAG → *nūru;* ZI → *napištu;*
1 → *ištēn*

Glossary

abālu "to bring": *t[u-ub-bal]* 64, *tu-ub-bal* 79,
abbūtu "intercession": *a-bu-ti* 99,
abku "captive": *ab-ka* 74,
abnu "stone; hail; glass, gem": NA_4 108,
abu "father": *a-bu-[šú]* 92,
abullu "(city) gate": KÁ.GAL 182,
adannu "term, deadline; period": *a-dan-ni-šú* 115, *a-dan-šú* 77,
adāru "to be dark, gloomy, afraid": *a-dir* 66, 86, *i'-da-ru* 41,
adnāti "world": *ad-[na]-a-ti* 149,
agû "wave, flood": *a-ge-e* 66, *a-gu-ú* 159,
ahāzu "to grasp, learn; (Š) to teach": *šu-hu-zu* 9,
ahu "brother": ŠEŠ.MEŠ-*šú* 93, 117,
aiu "which?": *a-a-ta* 175, *a-a-ú-tu* 174,
akālu "to eat, consume": *tak-kal* 157,
alaktu "way, behavior; traffic, business": *a-lak-tu* 138,
alāku "to go, (vent.) to come": *tal-li-ka* 44,
allāku "traveller": *al-la-ka* 139, *al-la-ki* 65,
altu "wife": *al-ti* 88,
ālû "townsman, fellow citizen": URU-*ú-šú* 135,
amāru "to see, behold, inspect, experience; to find, choose, select; (N) to appear, occur": *a-ma-ri* 76, *am-ra* 67, *in-na-[mar]* 10,
ana "to, for": *a-n]a* 196, *a-na* 2, 4, 7, 16, 52, 53, 65, 66, 77, 81, 85, 86, 88, 103, 104, 105, 109, 113, 117, 122, 132, 148, 152, 166, 187, *ana* 15, 21, 79, 178, *[a-na]* 53, 54, *[a]-na* 43, *[ana* 193,
anāhu "to be weary, exhausted; to become dilapidated; (Š) to make someone work hard; to worry": *šu-nu-hu* 45,
andullu "protection": *an-dùl-la-ka* 40,
anqullu "glow, fire": *an-qul-lu* 178,
anzanunzû "subterranean waters, abyss; water-table": *an-za-nu-un-ze-e* 70,
anzillu "abomination, taboo": *an-zil-li* 95,
apālu "to answer; to correspond": *ip-pa-lu* 93,
aplu "heir": IBILA-*šú* 116,
appu "nose, tip": *ap-pi* 131,
apsû "Abyss": *ap-si-i* 37, ABZU 57, 172,
apû "to shine forth; (Š) to make manifest, proclaim": *tu-šá-pi* 58,
arādu "to descend": *a-rid* 70, *ur-ra-du* 57, *ú-ri-du* 37,
arāmu "to envelop, cover": *e-ri-ma* 19,
arkatu "background, rear part": *ar-kàt-si-na* 152, *ar-[ka-a-t]ú* 78,
arku "long": *a-rik-tu₄* 59,
arnu "sin, guilt; penalty": *ar-na* 98,
arratu "curse": *[a]r-rat* 114,
aṣû "to go out, rise (sun)": *a-ṣi-ka* 15, *u-ṣu* 84,
ašābu "to sit, dwell": *áš-ba-ta* 151,
ašāšu "to be distressed, disturbed, worried": *ta-ta-šu-uš* 41,
aškuttu "(locking) bar, wedge": *áš-kut-ta* 183,
atāru "(D) to augment, increase; (Š) to increase, overdo": *li-[šá-tir* 192, *ut-tar* 100, 103, 119, *ut-[tar]* 106, *ú-šat-tar* 118,
atru "excessive": *at-ra* 113,
atta "you": *at-ta* 126, 159, 162, *at-ta-ma* 26, 34, 150, *at?-ta?* 73,
bā'iru "fisherman": LÚ.ŠU.HA 140,
bābilu see **lā bābil pāni**,
bābu "gate, doorway": *ba-a-bi* 13, *b[a-b]a* 168,
balāṭu "life": *ba-la-ṭi* 184, *ba-la-ṭ[u?* 119, TI.LA 100, 106,
balāṭu B "to live; (D) to keep alive, revive, heal": *tu-bal-laṭ* 80,
balu "without": *ba-li-ka* 45, 57,
banû "to create; (Š) id.": *ba-ni-tu₄* 192, *uš-tab-nu-ú* 24,
barīru "beam, ray": *ba-ri-ru-ka* 9,
barû "to inspect": *ta-bar-ri* 21,
barû see also **bitrû**
bārûtu "extispicy": *ba-ru-ti* 53, *ba-ru-ú-ti* 155,
bašû "to exist": *i-ba-áš-ši* 45,
bâ'u "to pass, go along, overtake, defeat": *i-ba-'u* 169, *i-ba-'u-ú* 172, *ta-ba-a'* 28, 30,
bêlu "to rule": *i-be-el* 116,
bēlūtu "lordship": *b]e-lut-ka* 192,
bēru "league": *bé-ri* 43,

bēru B "distant": *bé-ru-ti* 6, 19,

bêru "to examine, check": *te-bir-ši-na-ti* 127,

biltu "talent (weight), burden; tax, tribute": *bi-lat-su-nu* 196, *bil-ta* 115,

birbirru "sheen": *bir-bir-ru-ka* 37,

biri'u "medium (quality or measure)": *bi-ri-i* 113,

bitrû "to be(come) continuous, last, stay on; (Št) to persevere, continue": *tuš-ta-bar-ri* 42,

bītu "house": É 74, 200, É-*šú* 117,

bullû "to extinguish, terminate": *tu-bal-la* 95,

būlu "cattle; (wild) animals": MÁŠ.ANŠE 141,

būnzerru "snare": *bu-un-zer-ri* 142,

dabābu "to talk, prattle, blab, plot": *da-bi-bu* 167,

dābibu "speaker, talker": *da-bi-ba* 86,

dadmī "habitations": *da-ád-me* 153, 182, [*d*]*a-ád-me* 32,

daiānu see **dayānu**

dalālu "to praise": *i-dal-lal* 166,

dalāpu "to be sleepless": *dal-pa-ta* 44,

daltu "door": *da-lat* 182,

dannu "strong, hard, difficult": *dan-nu* 159,

dāmu "blood, resin": *da-mu* 84,

dāriš "forever": *da-riš* 166,

darû "to last, be everlasting": *da-ri*] 124, *da-*[*ri*] 121,

dārû "(ever)lasting, perpetual": *da-ri-i* 121,

dayānu "judge": *da-a-a-na* 101, *da-a-a-nu* 93, 97,

diānu "to pass judgment, judge": *i-di-nu* 101,

dīnu "(legal) case, judgment": *di-na* 62, *di-ni-šú* 92, *di-in* 63, 101, *di-in-šu-u*[*n*] 58, *di-in-šú* 127, *din-šu-un*] 62,

dipāru "torch": *d*]*i-pa-ri* 187,

dumqu "beauty, good luck": *dum-q*[*u*] 118, *dum-qí* 122,

dunnamû (person of low status): *dun-na-mu-ú* 132,

e'iltu "bond": *el-let-si-na* 163,

ebbu "clean": *e*]*b*$^{?}$*-bi* 58, *eb-bu-ú-ti* 160,

ebēru "to cross over": *e-bir* 66, *te-te-né-bir* 35,

ebru "comrade, friend": [*e-bir-šu*] 61,

edēšu "to be new; (D) to renew, restore, renovate, repair": *li-te-di-iš* 198,

edû "wave, flood, high water": *e-de-e* 69,

ēkallu "palace": É.GAL 102,

ekletu "darkness": *ek-le-ti* 17, 177, *ek-le-tu*$_4$ 2, 4,

eli "on, upon, over": UGU 100, 106, 119,

eliš "above, upward": *e-liš* 2, 4, 26,

ellu "pure, holy": *el-la* 157, *el-lu-ú-tu*$_4$ 160,

elû "to go up, arise, ascend; (Š) to raise, bring up": *tu-šel-li* 62, 70,

elû B "upper, high": *e-la-a-ti* 32, 33, *e-lu-ú-ti* 170,

emēdu "to lean on, support": *te-em-mi-id* 65, *te-mid* 77,

emūqu "strength; (pl.) armed forces, army": *e-mu-q*[*a-ka* 189,

enšu "weak, feeble": *en-še* 99, *en-šú* 133,

enû "to alter, change; (N) to be altered, revoked": *e-ni* 96, *in-nen-na-a* 82, *in-nen-nu-u* 64, 199,

ēnu "eye, eye-stone, spring": *i*$^{?}$-[*ni*$^{?}$*-šú*$^{?}$] 88, IGI.2-*ka* 154,

ēnu B "high priest": *e-nu* 195,

epēšu "to do, make, perform": *e-piš* 96, 107, 112, 122, *i-pu-šú* 124,

erbettu "group of four": *er-bet-ti* 12, LÍMMU.BA 152,

erbû "locust": *e-ri-ib* 172,

erēbu "to enter, come in": *ir-ru-bu* 117,

erēnu "cedar": GIŠ.EREN 53,

erpetu "cloud": DUNGU.MEŠ 168,

erṣetu "earth, underworld": *er-ṣe-ta* 21, 29, *er-ṣe-ti* 169, *er-ṣe-tu* 28, KI-*tì* 5, 87, 177, 178, 179, KI-[*tì*$^{?}$ 80

erû "copper": *e-re-e* 94,

ešēru "to be right, straight, thrive; (Št) to administer, regulate": *iš-šìr-šú* 91, *muš-te-še-ru* 98, *muš-te-šir* 34, *tuš-ta-šir*] 14, *tuš-te-eš-šir* 129, *tuš-te-šìr* 32, 151,

etēqu "to go past, proceed": *i-ti-qu* 138, *te-te-né-ti-iq* 27,

eṭemmu "spirit of the dead, ghost": *e-ṭém-mu* 145,

eṭūtu "darkness": *e-ṭ*[*u-t*]*i-šu-nu* 6, *e-ṭu-tu*$_4$ 176,

ezēbu "to leave; (Š) to save, rescue": *mu-še-zib* 91, *tu-še-zib* 69, 159,

ezzu "furious, angry": *ez-ze-ti* 48, *ez-zu* 150,

gamāru "to come to an end; to finish, annihilate, destroy; (D) to complete, end, abolish": *ú-gam-mar* 102,

gimru "total, totality, all": *gi-mir* 1, 3, 45, *gi-mir-ši-na* 16, 155, *gi-mir-šú-nu* 8,

ginâ "constantly, usually": *gi-na-a* 27, 30, 134,

gišparru "trap": *giš-par-ri-ka* 84,

hābilu "criminal, evildoer": *ha-bi-lu* 83, 103,

hadû "to be glad, rejoice; to be willing; to

wish": *ih-du-ú* 7,

halāqu "to disappear, run away, escape; (D) to cause to be lost, to destroy": *hal-qu* 145, *ú-hal-l*[*aq* 109, *ú-hal-laq* 104,

halpû "frost": *hal-pa-a* 181,

hamāṭu "to be quick; (Š) to do quickly": *tu-šah-maṭ* 126,

hamāṭu B "to burn (up); (Š) to set aglow": *mu-šah-miṭ* 18, 179, *tu-šah-miṭ* 42,

hanšā "fifty": *ha*]-*an-šá-a* 191,

harrānu "road": *har-ra-na-a-ti* 67, 72,

haṭṭu "scepter": GIŠ.NÍG.GIDRU 188,

hīdāti "joy": *hi-da-a-ti* 156,

hiṣbu "yield, abundance": *hi-ṣib* 197,

hubbulu "oppressed": *hu-ub-bu-lu* 133,

huhāru "trap": *hu-ha-ri* 94,

hurru "hole, ravine": *hur-ri* 132,

hurs/šānu "mountain": *hur-sa-a-ni* 21, 29, *hur-sa-a-nu* 174, *hur-šá-a-ni* 6,

iāti "me": *ia-a-ti* 148,

idû "to know": *i-de* 43, 94, *i-du-ú* 36, 72, [*ti*]-*i-de* 50,

ikribu "blessing": *ik-ri-bi-ši-na* 164,

illatu "mirth": *il-la-ta* 156,

ilu "god": DINGIR-*šú* 75, DINGIR.MEŠ 7, 46, 47, DINGIR.M[EŠ] 192,

imbāru "fog": *im-ba-ri* 39,

ina "in; from": *i-na* 73, 76, 89, 118, *ina* 10, 22, 37, 42, 45, 57, 62, 63, 69, 74, 80, 83, 84, 87, 92, 93, 94, 114, 115, 123, 125, 136, 137, 142, 144, 151, 156, 173, 185, 197, 198, 200, [*i-na* 56, [*in*]*a* 46,

īnu "eye" see **ēnu**,

išdu "foundation": *iš-da*?-*at* 188,

ištāru "goddess": ^{d}*iš-tar*.MEŠ 81,

ištēn "one": 1 105,

išû "to have": *i-ša-a* 168, *i*-[*ši*] 91,

itti "with": *it-ti-šú* 75,

izuzzu "to stand, be(come) present": *i-za-az-za* 92,

kabāsu "to tread upon, step, trample, subdue": *ú-kab-ba*-[*as*] 90, *ú-kab-bi-su* 170,

kabru "thick, heavy": [*kab-r*]*i* 118,

kakku "weapon": GIŠ.TUKUL-*ka-ma* 91,

kalāma "all, everything": *ka-la-ma* 146,

kališ "completely": *ka-liš* 13, 24,

kallatu "daughter-in-law, bride": *kal-la-ti* 200,

kalu "all, whole": *kal* 153, *ka-li-ši-na* 32,

kalû "to hold back, turn down": *tak-li* 147,

kamāru "hunting trap": *ka-ma-ru*?-[*ma*?] 87,

kamāsu "to kneel": *ik-kam-sa* 163, *kit-mu-sa* 15, 55, *kit-mu-su* 56, 131, [*kam-s*]*a-nik-ka* 51,

kânu "to be firm; (D) to set, establish": *kun-na-áš-šu* 90,

kapādu "to plan, scheme": *ik-pu-du* 162, *ka-pi-du* 96,

kaparru "shepherd boy": *ka-par-ri* 137,

kappu "drinking bowl": *kap-pa* 154,

kappu B "wing": *kap-pa* 70,

karābu "to bless": *ik-tar-ra-ba* 164, *ka-ra-bu* 130,

karû "to be short; (D, Š) to shorten": *tu-š*[*ak-ri*] 59, *ú-kar*$_5$-*ri* 89,

kaspu "money, price; silver": *kàs-pa* 103, 105,

kasû "to bind": *ka-sa-ta* 39,

kaṣābu "to reduce; (Št) to cause a decrease": *uš-ta-kaṣ-ṣa-ab* 109, *uš-ta-kaṣ-ṣab* 104,

kaṣāru "to bind, tie, knot; to organize; to construct; to prepare": *ka-ṣir* 95, *šuk-ṣu-ru* 129,

kašādu "to reach, arrive at; to catch up with; to achieve, get; to conquer, vanquish; (Š) to cause to achieve; to chase away, pursue": *i-kaš-šad-su* 114, *tu-šak-šad* 162,

katāmu "to cover, veil": [*ká*]*t-ma-ta* 39,

kāru "quay, port, harbour, trade colony": *ka-a-ri* 157,

kāti "you": *ka-a-ta* 46,

kātimtu "net": *ka-tim-ti* 140,

kî "as; if, whether": *ki-i* 30, GIM 168,

kibrāti "regions, horizons": *kib-ra-a-ti* 194, *kib-ra-a-tu*$_4$ 175, *kib-rat* 12,

kibsu "footprint; path": *ki-bi-is-si-na* 10, 50,

kīma "like, as; when, after, if": *ki-ma* 5, 12, 39, 46, 60, 121, 179, GIM 168, [*k*]*i-ma* 39

kimtu "kin, family": *kim-ta* 120, *kim-ta-šú* 135,

kīnāti "righteousness, loyalty": *ki-na-a-ti* 63,

kīnu "just, innocent, true, righteous, honest": *ke-e-nù* 56, *ki-i-ni* 58, 110, *ki-i-nu*] 60, *ki-na-a-ti* 63, *ki-nu* 118,

kipdu "plan": *kip-di-ši-na* 50,

kippatu "circle, disc, loop, circumference": *kip-pat* 22,

kippu "snare": *kip-pu* 90,

kīsu "money bag": *ki-i-si* 108, *ki-i-sa*] 109, *ki-si* 69, KUŠ.NÍG.NA$_4$ 104, 139,

kiššatu "world, universe; full flood": *kiš-šá-ti* 34, 46,

kullatu "entirety": *kul-lat* 14, *kul-lat-si-na* 23, 51,

kullumu "to show, display": *tu-kal-lam* 71, 72,

97, *tu-kal-lam-šú* 74,

kurnugû "netherworld": KUR.NU.GI$_4$.A 80,

kurunnu "date beer or wine": *ku-ru-un-n*[*a*] 161, *ku-ru-un-ši-na* 157,

kussû "throne, chair": *ku-us-si-i* 188,

kuṣṣu "cold, winter": *ku-ṣu* 181,

lā "not": *la* 36, 43, 67, 72, 85, 86, 89, 98, 99, 114, 115, 122, 148, 168, 174, 175, 199, [*la*] 80,

lā bābil pāni "merciless, unforgiving"**:** *la ba-bil pa-ni* 184,

labānu "to stroke (the nose)": *la-ban* 131,

labāšu "to dress; (Gt) to clothe oneself, (stat.) be clothed in; (Š) to cover": *lit-bu-šu* 174, *mu-šal-biš* 181,

lamû "to surround, besiege": *la-mu-ú* 61, *la-mu-ši-na-a-ti* 159,

lapātu "to touch, strike, affect, afflict, infect": *la-pit* 84,

libbu "heart": *lìb-ba*$^{?}$] 66, *lì*]*b*$^{?}$*-ba-k*[*a* 191, *lìb-bi-šá* 36,

lišānu "tongue, language": *li-šá-na* 167, *li-šá-nu* 49,

lithušu "whispered prayer": *lit-hu-ša* 131,

lumnu "evil": *lum-nu* 124,

maʾādu "to be much": *ma-aʾ-da* 110, 111,

mahāru "to accept, receive; to appeal to, petition; to match, equal, correspond": *i-mah-har-ka* 134, 136, 138, 140, 142, 144, *im-hu-ru-ka* 146, 147, *ma-hir* 98, 99, *ta-mah-har* 158, *tam-ta-har* 164, *tam-tah-har* 160,

māhāzu "cult centre, (holy) city": *ma-ha-zi* 71,

māhiru "opponent; supplicant": *ma-hi-ru* 68,

māhiṣu "archer; beater": *ma-hi-ṣu* 141,

mahru "front; before": *ma-har-ka* 55, *mah-ri-ka* 125, 173, *ma*]*h-ri-ka* 56, *mah-r*[*i-k*]*a* 196, *mah-ri-ka*] 123,

maiālu "bed, resting place": KI.NÁ 200,

mākaltu (wooden dish or saucer): *ma-kal-ti* 53, 155,

makkūru "property": NÍG.GA-*šú* 116,

mala "as much/many as; all, everything that": *ma-la* 154, 155,

malku "king, sovereign, prince"*:* *ma-al-ki* 31, *ma-al-ku* 7, *mal-ku* 24,

malû "to be full, fill(ed) up": *im-lu-ú* 20, *ma-lu-ú* 171,

māmītu "oath": *ma-mi-ti-ka* 85,

mamma(n) "somebody, anybody": *ma-am-ma* 128, [*mam-ma*]-*an* 189,

manāma "somebody": *ma-na-ma* 128,

mannu "who?": [*man*$^{?}$*-nu*$^{?}$] 57,

manû "counted": *ma-n*[*u-ti*] 43,

marṣu "difficult; sick person, patient": LÚ.GI[G 77,

masdaru "regularly, always": *mas-da-ra* 134, *mas-da-ri* 123,

maṣû "to match, reach": *im-ṣa-a* 155, *im-ṣu-ú* 154,

maštaku "living quarters, chamber, cell": *maš-ta-ki-šá* 200,

mātu "land, country": *ma-a-ti* 47, *ma-a-tu*$_4$ 48, *ma-ta-a-ti* 197, KUR.KUR 20, 22, 23, 49, KUR.K[UR] 16, KUR.MEŠ 155, 170, [KU]R.KUR 40, KUR 18, KUR$^{?}$ 198,

mayālu see **maiālu**

mê "water, juice, sap, bodily fluids": A.MEŠ 121,

melammu "nimbus, radiance": *mé-lam-mu-ka* 11,

mērēšu "cultivated land, cultivation": *me-reš* 18,

mēseru "imprisonment": *mé-se-ra* 97,

mešrû "wealth": *meš-ra-a* 120,

mihirtu "produce, income": *mi-hir-ti* 173,

milku "advice, counsel": *mil-k*[*u*] 186,

mīlu "flood": ILLU 29,

mimma "anything": *mim-ma* 111,

mīnâ "what?": *mi-na-a* 103,

mīšaru "justice": *me-šá-ri* 101,

mithāriš "each one, equally, together": *mit-ha-riš* 25,

mithartu "unanimity, consensus": *mit-har-tu*$_4$ 52,

mitluku "counsel": *mit-lu-ku* 186,

mītu "dead": *mi-i-tu*$_4$ 80, 145,

mizʾu "sweet beer": *mi-zi-iʾ-ši-na* 161,

mūdû "knowledgeable": *mu-du-ú* 122,

mukarrû "who shortens": [*m*]*u-kar-ru-ú* 180,

munnabtu "fugitive, refugee": *mu-un-nab-tú* 71,

munnarbu "runaway": *mun-nar-bi* 71,

murriku "who prolongs": *mu-ur-ri-ku* 180,

murtappidu "roving": *mur-tap-pi-du* 145,

mussû "to identify, distinguish, (re)locate": *tu-mas-si* 127,

muṣallû "one who prays": *mu-ṣal-lu-ú* 143,

mūšabu "dwelling": *mu-šab-šú* 102

mušaddinu "who exacts payment": *mu-šad-din* 113,

mušahlû "who lightens": *mu-šah-li* 2, 4, *mu-šah-lu-ú* 178,

mušakṣibu "who reduces": *mu-šak-ṣib* 184,

mušēlû "who lifts": *mu-še-lu-u* 183,
mušemmû "roasting pot": *mu-šem-mi* 54,
mušēridu "who sends down": *mu-še-rid* 178,
mušītu "night(-time)": GE_6.MEŠ 180,
muškēnu "poor man, beggar, commoner": *muš-ke-nu* 133,
mušnammiru "illuminator": *muš-na-mir* 1, 3, 17, 176, 177,
mušpalkû "who opens wide": *muš-pal-ku-u* 182,
mušpardû "shining, bright": *muš-par-du-ú* 176,
muštālu "judicious, circumspect, deliberate": *muš-ta-*lu_4 101,
muštēnû "who changes": *muš-te-nu-ú* 108, *muš-ten-nu-ú* 123,
mūšu "night": *mu-ši-im-ma* 42, *mu-šá* 44,
muterru "who returns": *mu-ter* 105, *mu-ter-ru* 141,
muttaggišu "bandit": *mut-tag-gi-šú* 144,
muttahlilu "creep": *mut-tah-li-lu* 143,
mūtu "death": *mu-ú-t[i]* 185, *mu-ú-[tu]* 89,
nablu "flame, flash": *nab-li* 179,
nadānu "to give": *na-din* 103, 105, 113, 118, *ta-din* 147, *ta-nam-din-ši-na-[ti]* 150, *ta-nam-di[n* 66,
nadû "to throw, cast": *na-du-ú* 74,
nagbu "spring, fountain, source": *nag-bi* 121,
nâhu "to rest, calm down": *nu-uh* 200,
nakru "strange, foreign, hostile; enemy": LÚ.KÚR 137,
namirtu "illumination": *na-mir-ta* 175, *na-mir-ti* 10,
namrirru "brilliance": *nam-ri-ru-ka* 20,
namru "bright, radiant": *nam-ri* 193,
namurratu "terrifying splendour, brilliance": *[n]a-mur-rat-ka* 48,
namzāqu "key": *nam-za-qí* 183,
napalkû "to be wide; (Š) to open up": *tuš-pal-ki* 13,
napardû "to shine; (Š) to brighten": *tuš-par-di* 6,
napāšu "to breathe": *i-nap-pu-u[š* 60,
napharu "totality, sum, all, whole, entirety": *nap-har* 46, 49,
napištu "life": *na-piš-ti* 25, *na-piš-[ti]* 18, ZI-tì 59,
napšatu "life": *nap-šá-a-*tu_4 78,
naptanu "meal, dinner": *nap-tan* 194,
nāqidu "herdsman": *na-qid-si-na* 26, *na-qí-du* 33, 137,
naqû "to libate, pour out": *i-naq-qa-nik-ka* 158,
nāru "river": ÍD 173,
nasāhu "to pull out, uproot; to extract; to remove": *is-su*[?]*-uh* 77,
našû "to lift, carry, bring": *iš-šu-ú* 88, *liš-šu-ka* 196, *na-áš* 69, 139,
naṭālu "to look, see": *i-na-aṭ-ṭa-lu* 38, *na-aṭ-la-a-ta* 50,
nebû "to shine": *n[é-bi-ma]* 187,
nēmelu "profit": *né-me-li-im-ma* 109, *né-me-li-ma* 104,
nesû "to be far away, distant": *né-su-ú* 135,
nesû B "far(away), distant, remote": *né-su-ti* 43,
nindabû "cereal offering": NIDBA.MEŠ-*šú-n[u* 14,
niqû "offering": *ni-qé-e* 197, *ni-qí-i* 151,
nišē "people": UN.MEŠ 2, 4, 23, 81, 114, 187, UN.MEŠ-šú 79,
nīšu "lifting": *ni-ši* 88,
niṭlu "sight, look, glance, gaze": *ni-ṭi-il* 154,
nūru "light, lamp": *nu-úr* 34, *nu-úr-ka* 38, *nu-ri-[ka* 16, *nu-ú-ru* 74, ZÁLAG-*ka* 52, 150,
pahāru "to gather, rally, get together": *ip-hu-ru* 47,
palāhu "to fear, be afraid, worry; to respect, revere, venerate; to serve": *i-pal-la-hu* 85, *pal-ha-ka* 165,
palû "reign, dynasty": *pa-le-e* 188,
pānu "face, presence": *pa-na* 64, 168, *pa-ni* 184, *pa-n[u]-ka* 41,
pānu B (a measure) PI 118,
paqādu "to appoint, assign; to review, check; (D) to entrust": *paq-da-ka* 24, *pu-uq-qu-du* 128, *ta-paq-qid* 23, 31,
parakku "throne dais": *pa-rak-ka-ka* 198, *[pa-rak-ki]* 13,
parāsu "to decide": *ta-par-ra-as* 78, 152,
pâru "to search for": *pa-ru-ka* 150,
pašāru "to solve, explain; to dissolve; to convert": *ta-pa-áš-šar* 126,
pāširu "interpreter, explainer": *pa-še-ru* 54,
paṭāru "to release, loosen": *ta-pat-ṭar* 129, 163, *ta-paṭ-ṭár* 73,
petû "to open; (ŠD) to open up": *pe-tu-u* 17, *pe-tu-ú* 177, 182, *tuš-pat-ti* 76, 149, 153,
pû "mouth, utterance, command": *pi-i* 93, *pi-i-ka* 82, *pi-i-šú* 132, *pi-i-šú-nu* 125, 126, *pi-šú* 199,
puluhtu "fear": *pu-luh-ta* 171, *pu-luh-ti* 138,

puzru "shelter": *pu-uz-ru* 9, *pu-uz-ra-at* 73,
qablu "middle (parts), loins": *qab-lu* 178,
qablu B "battle, warfare": *qa-bal* 185,
qabû "to say": *liq-bi-ka* 200, *taq-bu-u-[ši-na-ti]* 63,
qaqqaru "ground": *qaq-qar-šu* 96,
qarnu "horn": *qar-na-šú* 95,
qâšu "to give, bestow": *qí-šá-áš-šú* 111, *ta-qiš* 147,
qātu "hand; responsibility (of)": *qa-tuk-ka* 128,
qerbu "inside": *qé-reb* 22, 36,
qibītu "command": *qí-bit* 82, 199,
qû "filament": *qé-e* 39,
rabû "(to be) great; (Š) to glorify": GAL-*ti* 200, *li-šar-[bu-ú* 190,
raggu "evil": *rag-gu* 56, *rag-g[u* 59,
rapāšu "to be wide, extensive; (D) to extend, expand, enlarge, increase": *ú-rap-pa-áš* 120,
rappu "bridle, pole; hoop, clamp": *rap-pu* 87,
rapšu "wide, extensive": *rap-šu* 40, *ra-pa-áš-tu₄* 179, DAGAL-tu₄ 35, DAGAL-tì 169, 177,
rašû "to get, obtain, acquire": *i-ra-áš-š[i]* 120, *i-raš-ši* 115,
râšu "to rejoice": *i-riš-šu-ka* 8, *re-šá-ta* 156,
re'û "to shepherd": *te-re-'e* 25,
rē'û "shepherd": *re-'u-u* 33, *re-'u-ú* 136,
redû "to lead": *ir-te-du-ú* 173, UŠ.MEŠ-*di* 68,
rehû "to pour in, imbue, impregnate": *i-re-eh-hi-šu-ma* 60,
riksu "setup; bond, agreement, obligation; tie": *ri-kis* 53, *rik-sa-a-ti* 55,
rubû "ruler, prince": *ru-bu-u* 195, NUN.MEŠ 102,
ruggugu "villainous": *rug-gu-gu* 127,
rūqu "distant": *ru-qat* 135, SUD.MEŠ 105,
sābi'u "barkeeper, brewer": *sa-bi-'i* 158, *se-bi-'i-i* 157,
sahāpu "to overwhelm": *sa-hi-ip* 40, 94, *sah-pat* 48, *sah-pu* 5, *ta-sah-hap* 83,
sahāru "to turn, go around, return; to seek, look for": *ta-sah-ra* 44,
saklu "barbarous": *sak-la-a-ti* 167,
salāmu "to make peace; (D) to reconcile": *t]u-sal-lam* 75, *[t]u-sal-lam* 81,
sâqu "to be narrow; (D) to constrict, give a hard time": *t]u-saq* 59,
sattakku "constantly": *sat-tak-ku* 9,
sihpu "surface, cover, overlay, bark": *se-he-ep* 153, *si-hi-ip* 20,
sikkatu "pin": *sik-ka-ta* 183,
sikkūru "lock": *sik-kur* 182,
sirqu "offering of aromatics": *sír-qé-ši-na* 160,
sullû "supplication": *su-la-a* 130,
sulû "street, track, trail": *su-le-e* 144, *[s]u-li-i* 68,
suppû "prayer": *su-up-pa-a* 130,
sūtu "seah, a dry measure": GIŠ.BÁN 112,
ṣabātu "to seize, take hold of, conceive, capture, arrest; (Gt) to be seized, held, tied up": *ṣa-bi-tú* 99, *ṣa-bit* 107, 110, 112, *ti-iṣ-bu-tú* 62,
ṣaiādu "hunter": *ṣa-a-a-du* 141,
ṣā'idu "roaming about, restless": *ṣa-'i-da* 67,
ṣālilu "sleeper": *ṣa-li-li* 60,
ṣaliptu "deception": *ṣa-l[íp-ti]* 167, *[ṣa]-lip-[ti]* 122,
ṣalpu "rogue, roguish, false": *ṣal-pa* 61, 97, *ṣal-pa-a-[ti]* 86,
ṣerretu "breast, tit, udder": *ṣer-ret* 17,
ṣēru "open country, plain, steppe": EDIN 73, 136, 144,
ṣētu "heat, light, shine": UD.DA-*ka* 10, 175,
ṣibittu "imprisonment": *ṣi-b[ít-ti]* 74,
ṣibtu "interest (on money, silver)": *ṣib-ti* 103,
ṣiliptu "treachery, lying": *ṣi-l[ip-ti]* 112, *ṣi-lip-ti* 107,
ṣīru "emissary, envoy; exalted": *ṣi-ra-ta-ma* 82,
ṣītu "rising, sunrise; exit": *ṣi-it* 126, *[ṣ]i-tuk-ka* 47,
ṣummirtu "wish, desire": *ṣu-um-mi-rat* 162
ṣummuru "to desire, long for": *ṣu-um-mu-rat* 52,
ša "that; what; of; who, which": *ša* 32, *šá* 6, 13, 14, 24, 26, 43, 44, 45, 46, 55, 61, 62, 63, 65, 67, 68, 72, 73, 74, 75, 77, 85, 88, 94, 95, 101, 110, 127, 129, 135, 143, 149, 159, 167, 168, 171, 172, 173, 174, 175, 199, *[š]a*? 49, *[šá* 58, *[šá]* 36,
šā'ilu "dream interpreter": *šá*-DINGIR.MEŠ 54,
šabsu "angry": *[š]ab-sa-tu₄* 81,
šadlu "broad, wide": *šá-di-il-ta* 35,
šadû "mountain": *šá-di-i* 19, KUR-*i* 39,
šahānu "to be(come) warm": *iš-tah-ha-nu* 175, *[iš-ta-ah-na]* 12,
šakānu "to place, set; (Š) to provide with": *šá-k[in* 123, *šá-kin* 125, *šak-na* 25, *tu-šá-áš-kan* 70,
šakkanakku "governor, viceroy": *ša]k-ka-nak-ku* 195,
šalāmu see **salāmu**,
šalgu "snow, sleet": *šal-gi* 181,

šallu "prisoner, deportee": *šal-la* 72, 185,

šâlu "to ask, question": *i*[*š*]-*šá-al* 115,

šalummatu "splendor": *šá-lum-mat-ka* 19,

šamallû "trading agent, apprentice": LÚ.ŠÁMAN.LÁ 139,

šamāmu "heaven": *šá-ma-mu* 154, *šá-ma-mi* 1, 3, 27, 29, *šá-m*[*a-mi*] 17, [*šá-ma-mi*] 11,

šamāru "to extol, pray": *iš-tam-ma-ra* 165,

šamšu "sun": ^{d}UTU-*ši* 143, ^{d}[UTU]-*ši* 68,

šamru "fierce": *šam-ru* 150,

šamû "heaven": AN-*e* 22, 182,

šanānu "to rival, vie": *šá-ni-in* 189,

šapālu "to be low, humble; (D) "to lower, humiliate": *ú-šap-pal* 108,

šapāru "to send (word), to write": *ta-š*[*ap-par*] 67,

šaplāti "lower parts, nether world": *šap-la-a-ti* 31, 33, 123,

šapliš "below, down, downwards": *šap-liš* 2, 4, 26,

šaqālu "to weigh, balance": *šaq-la-a-ta* 22,

šaqû "to be(come) high, elevated, to move upward, upstream; (D) to raise up, high": *ú-šaq-qa* 108,

šarāku "to present, endow": *šá-ri-ku* 184,

šarrāqu "thief": *šar-ra-qu* 143,

šarru "king": LUGAL 24, [LUGAL 195,

šarrūtu "kingship, kingdom": LU[GAL-*ú-ti*] 188,

šāru "wind; direction": IM 152,

šarūru "radiance, ray": *šá-ru-ru-ka* 5, 174,

šasû "to call, shout": *i-šá-as-si-ka* 132,

šāt urri "morning": *šat ur-ri* 18,

šatû "to drink": *ta-šat-ti* 157, 161,

še'u "grain, kernel": ŠE-*im* 18, 118,

še'û "to seek, strive for; (Gtn) to frequent": *iš-te-né-'u-ú* 11, *ta-še-'e-e* 78,

šelaltu "three": *še-lal-*[*ti*] 105,

šemû "to hear, heed": *ta-šem-me* 130, [*t*]*a-šem-me* 127, *tal-te-me* 146,

šērtu "morning": *še-re-e-ti* 187,

šētu "net, web": *še-et-ka* 87,

šiddu "long side, length: stretch, reach": *šid-di* 43, 96, 105,

šikāru "beer": *ši-kar* 157, 158,

šīmtu "fate, destiny": *ši-ma-ti* 89,

šina "they": *ši-na* 166, *ši-na-ma* 165,

šiqlu "shekel": GÍN 105,

šīqu "a capacity measure": *ši-qa-a-ti* 113,

šittu "sleep": *šit-ta* 60,

šitūltu "deliberation": *ši-tul-ta* 186,

šubtu "seat, settlement; ambush": *šu-bat* 102, 193,

šukênu "prostration": *šu-ken-na* 131,

šumdulu "extensive, vast": [*š*]*u-um-dul-ta* 28,

šumu "name": *šu-mi-ka* 86, *šum-šú* 111,

šunnû "double": *šu-un-na-a* 49,

šunu "they": *šu-nu* 93, 117,

šupšuqu "difficult, trying": *šup-šu-qat* 65,

šūpû "illustrious": *šu-pu-u* 64,

šurīpu "ice, frost": *šu-ri-pa* 181,

šurru "to bend forwards, peer": *šu-ra-ta* 21,

šūrubtu "terror, awe, dread": *šu-ru-bat* 136,

šuškallu "net": *šu-uš-kal-li-ka* 83, *šu-uš-kal-lu* 5,

šutēpuru "to hasten, bestir o.s.": *uš-te-ep-*[*pe-r*]*a* 16,

šuttu "dream": MÁŠ.GE_6.MEŠ 54,

šūt "those of": *šu-ut* 25, 38, 49, 124, 125, 147, 163, 164, 169, 170, 171,

šūturu "excellent": *šu-tu-ru* 46,

takkassu "block (of stone), (unfinished) piece": *ták-kàs-si* 30,

tāmartu "appearance": *ta-mar-ti-ka* 7,

tamkāru "merchant, trader; investor, banker": LÚ.DAM.GÀR 69, 139,

tāmtu "sea": *ta-ma-tu*$_4$ 35, A.AB.BA 29, 38, 66, 171, 172,

tappû "comrade, companion, partner, friend": *tap-pe-e-šú* 88,

tarāṣu "to stretch out, spread out": *tar-ṣa-at* 87,

tarbītu "greatness": *tar-ba-ti-ka* 166,

târu "to return; (D) to turn back": *ta-r*]*i* 80, *tu-tar-ra* 61,

tašīltu "glory, splendour": *ta-ši-la-ti-ka* 193,

tenēšētu "mankind": *te-né-še-e-ti* 15, 51,

têrtu "omen": *te-re-te-ši-na* 129, 151, *te-r*[*e-t*]*i* 76,

tēšû "anarchy, confusion": *te-še-e* 137, 185,

ṭa'tu "gift, bribe": *ṭa-a'-ti* 98, 99,

ṭâbu "to be good": *ṭa-a-ab* 119, *ṭa-a-bi* 100, 106,

ṭēmu "order, report, mind; mood, disposition": *ṭ*]*è-me* 186,

u "and": *u* 2, 4, 7, 26, 43, 44, 56, 58, 59, 168, 190, 195, ù 130, 131, 156,

û see **še'u**

uklu "darkness": *uk-li* 176, [*uk-l*]*a* 42,

ul "not": *u*[*l* 124, *ul* 41, 64, 82, 84, 91, 92, 93, 94, 116, 117, 147, 154, 155, 189, [*u*]*l* 45

ulālu "feeble-minded, imbecile": *ú-la-lu* 133,

ulla "no!": *ul-la* 125,

ūmišam "daily": *u*$_4$*-mi-šam* 28, 30,

ūmišamma "every day": *u*$_4$*-me-šam-ma* 41,

ummânu "investor, creditor": *um-ma-ni* 118,

ummisalla "daily(?)": *um-mi-sal-la* 134,

ūmu "day": *u*$_4$*-me* 178, 180, *u*$_4$*-me-šú* 114, *u*$_4$*-mu* 178, *u*$_4$*-um* 89, UD-20-KÁM 156,

uppu "socket": *up-pi* 183,

urhu "road": *ú-r*[*u-uh-šú*] 65,

urru "day, daylight": *ur-ra* 44, *ur-ri* 18, see also *šāt urri,*

usandû "fowler": LÚ.MUŠEN.DÙ 142,

usātu "help, assistance": *ú-sa-at* 122,

uznu "ear, understanding": GEŠTU.2-*ši-na* 149, *uz-na-ši-na* 76, *uz-ni-ši-na* 153,

yāti see **iāti**

zabālu "to carry, bear; (Š) to make bear, suffer": *tu-šá-az-bal* 98,

zakāru "to pronounce, invoke": *za-kir* 86,

zakû "to be clean; (D) to purify": [*tu-zak-ka* 62,

zāmânû "hostile; enemy": *za-ma-né-e* 58,

zenû "to be angry": [*ze-nu-ú*] 75,

zēru "seed, offspring": NUMUN-[*šú*] 121, NUMUN-*šú-nu* 124,

zēru B "hated": *ze-ru* 90,

zêru "to hate": *ta-zer-ši-na-ti* 148,

zibānītu "scales": *zi-ba-ni-ti* 107, 110,

zikru "name; utterance, command": MU-*ka* 190, *zi-kir-k*[*a*] 165, *zik-ru-ka* 64,

zīqu "draft, breeze": *ziq* 18

Index of Names

Divine Names

Temple Names

Place Names

SIGN LIST

No.	Value	Count
	x	55
001	*ina*	35
002	*hal*	4
005	*ba*	27
	BA	6
006	*zu*	2
006.128	ABZU	2
007	*su*	12
	KUŠ	2
008	*rug*	1
009	*bal*	6
	pal	5
010	*ád*	3
012	*tar*	10
	šel	2
	ṭar	2
	kut	1
013	d	38
	DINGIR	7
	an	7
	AN	2
015	*ka*	85
035	*nag*	1
	naq	1
	nak	1
038	URU	1

No.	Value	Count
053	*šah*	7
055	*la*	53
	LA	2
057	*mah*	12
058	*tu*	33
059	*li*	25
	le	5
060	KÚR	1
061	*mu*	40
	MU	1
062	*qa*	6
063	*kát*	1
064	*kàt*	1
068	*ru*	36
	šup	1
069	*miṭ*	3
	mit	3
	bat	3
	be	3
	bít	1
	mid	1
070	*na*	110
071	*šir*	3
072	*kul*	3
	NUMUN	2
	zer	2
	qul	1

No.	Sign	Value	Count
073		*ti*	83
		TI	2
074		*mas*	3
		bar	2
		BAR	1
		BÁN	1
		maš	1
075		*nu*	37
		NU	1
076		MÁŠ	2
077		*kun*	1
078		*hu*	10
		paq	3
		MUŠEN	1
079		*nam*	5
080		*ek*	4
		ik	4
		iq	1
081		*mut*	2
083		*rat*	5
084		*zi*	5
		ze	4
		ZI	1
085		*gi*	11
		ge	1
086		*ri*	40
		re	10
		dal	2
		tal	2
087		*nun*	1
		zil	1
		NUN	1
088		*kab*	3
		kap	2
094		*tì*	9
		tim	1
095		*mun*	1
099		*en*	3
103		INNIN	1
104		*sa*	15
112		*si*	15
		se	3
114		*ṭár*	1
115		*šak*	5
		riš	3
		šaq	2
		reš	1
		saq	1
		sak	1
123		*dir*	2
124		*tap*	2
		tab	1
124,42		LÍMMU	1
126		*tak*	3

No.	Value	Count
	taq	1
	šum	1
	tag	1
128	AB	5
	ab	3
	ap	2
129	*nap*	5
	nab	2
130	*uk*	2
	uq	1
131	*as*	4
	az	2
133	KÁ	1
134	*um*	6
139	*ta*	72
142	*i*	61
142a	*ia*	1
143	*kan*	1
	KÁM	1
144.211	IBILA	1
145	*at*	12
	aṭ	2
	ad	1
147	*ṣi*	7
	ṣe	4
148	*in*	9
149	*rap*	3
151	LUGAL	3
152	*šir*	3
	hir	3
	šar	3
166	*raš*	1
167	*qab*	1
168	EDIN	3
169	*tah*	3
170	*am*	2
172	*bil*	2
	ṭè	1
190	*ziq*	1
	zik	1
191	*qu*	5
192	*kàs*	3
	kaṣ	2
203	*úr*	2
205	*il*	3
206	*du*	16
207	tu_4	16
	dum	2
208	ANŠE	1
211	*uš*	8
	UŠ	1
212	*iš*	10
	mil	1
214	*bi*	22

No.	Sign	Value	Count	No.	Sign	Value	Count
		bé	3	306		*ub*	3
		kaš	1			*up*	2
215		*šem*	3	307		*mar*	3
		rik	2	308		*e*	41
228		*kib*	3	309		*lut*	1
		kip	3	312		*un*	8
229		NA$_4$	3			UN	7
230		*qaq*	1	313		*sah*	4
		DÙ	1			*kit*	4
231		*ni*	20			*qid*	3
		né	11			*líl*	1
		ṣal	4	314		*šid*	3
232		*er*	5			*rid*	2
		ir	2			*laq*	2
233		*mal*	1			*ret*	1
237		DAGAL	3			*šit*	1
280		*ták*	1			*lak*	1
295		*pa*	25	318		*ú*	52
		GIDRU	1			*šam*	4
295k		*šap*	8	319		GA	1
		šab	2	321		*luh*	2
296		GIŠ	5			*làh*	1
		is	3	322		*kal*	11
		ez	2			*dan*	3
		iṣ	1			*reb*	2
		giš	1			*líp*	1
298		*al*	6			*tan*	1

No.	Sign	Value	Count
324	𒂍	É	6
		bit	5
		é	2
		bet	1
		pit	1
326	𒄄	GI_4	1
328	𒊏	*ra*	25
		RA	2
329	𒇯	*dùl*	1
330	𒇽	LÚ	7
331	𒋀	ŠEŠ	2
332	𒍠	*zak*	1
333	𒃼	GÀR	2
		qar	2
334	𒀉	*it*	2
		id	1
		et	1
335	𒁕	*da*	23
		ṭa	6
		DA	2
339	𒀾	*áš*	12
342	𒈠	*ma*	64
343	𒃲	GAL	3
346	𒄫	*piš*	6
		kir	2
		biš	1
347	𒈩	*mir*	13
349	𒁓	*bur*	1
353	𒊭	*ša*	4
354	𒋗	*šu*	42
		qat	2
		ŠU	1
355	𒇻	*lip*	3
		nar	1
362	𒃵	*gam*	1
366	𒆳	KUR	18
		lat	5
		šat	4
		šad	3
		sat	1
		mat	1
		laṭ	1
		maṭ	1
		kur	1
367	𒊺	*še*	16
		ŠE	2
371	𒁍	*bu*	14
		pu	12
		sír	1
372	𒊻	*uz*	4
		us	1
373	𒋤	SUD	1
374	𒈲	*muš*	13
		ṣer	1

		ṣir	1
375		*ter*	2
		tir	1
376		*te*	28
		ten	1
377		*kar*	3
378		*liš*	9
381		UTU	20
		ut	15
		u_4	8
		par	7
		tú	4
		UD	3
		tam	3
		BABBAR	2
		lah	1
383		*pi*	11
		pe	5
		PI	1
		GEŠTU	1
384		*lìb*	3
393		ZÁLAG	2
		ṣab	1
395		*zib*	3
		ṣib	3
396		*hi*	8
		he	1
397		*ʾu*	5
		ʾa	4
		ʾi	3
		ʾe	2
		iʾ	2
		aʾ	2
398		*uh*	3
		ih	1
		ah	1
		eh	1
399		*im*	10
		em	1
		IM	1
399.123		DUNGU	1
400		*bir*	6
401		*har*	15
		hur	5
		mur	2
406		*kam*	2
411		*u*	22
412		UGU	3
420		*lit*	2
		let	2
425		*kiš*	2
		kis	1
		qiš	1
427		*mi*	19

No.	Value	Count
	mé	2
	GE_6	2
428	ŠÁMAN	1
431	NÁ	1
433	*num*	2
	nù	1
435	*lam*	7
439	*ban*	1
440	*kim*	2
	ṭém	1
	GIM	1
441	*ul*	18
446	GIG	1
449	*ši*	33
	IGI	1
451	*ar*	4
455	*ù*	3
457	*di*	17
	de	4
	ṭi	2
459	*dul*	1
	tul	1
461	*ki*	25
	qí	8
	KI	7
	qé	5
	ke	2
465	*din*	9
467	*dun*	1
468	*kù*	1
469	*pat*	5
	paṭ	3
	PAD	1
	šuk	1
471	*man*	1
	20	1
	mam	1
472	*eš*	1
480	*gì*	10
	ana	5
	01	1
481	*lal*	2
	LÁ	1
483	*hap*	1
532	*me*	15
533	MEŠ	26
	meš	1
535	*ip*	5
	ep	2
	eb	2
	ib	1
536	*ku*	13
	tuš	10
	TUKUL	1

No.	Value	Count
537	*lu*	18
538	*kin*	2
	ken	1
541	EREN	1
545	*šú*	36
554	*šal*	4
	sal	3
	rak	2
	rag	2
	mim	1
555	*ṣu*	7
556	*nen*	3
557	DAM	2
559	*gu*	5
563	*nik*	2
564	*el*	4
565	*lum*	2
	lu$_4$	1
570	2	2
574	*tuk*	2
575	*ur*	4
	liq	1
579	*a*	110
	A	7
579.322	ILLU	1
582	ÍD	1
586	*ṣa*	12
	za	6
589	*ha*	8
	HA	1
592	*sik*	2
595	*ṭu*	3
	GÍN	1
597	*šá*	79
	NÍG	4
	gar	1
598a	*í*	5